Testimonials

I attribute many of my successes as a mom to the skills I have learned from my mom, Edwina. Children are a gift! And being a parent is a gift too. The wisdom shared in this book will change your approach to parenting and allow you to interact with your child in a way that brings out the best in him or her. It will inspire you with ideas on how to make your parenting journey one that is purposed and fun. Thank you, Edwina, for caring so much about children and for taking the time to write this book that will be a wonderful resource for parents!

—Lakisha Yirenkyi, parent, art teacher, and singer

My sister, Edwina, has always been a teacher, and I was her very first student. She was a few years older than I and began teaching me the basics of education when I was barely four years old. I entered school wondering why all the other students were so behind. If only they'd had a sister like mine.

So, it came as no surprise that she would be an excellent educator of young children for much of her life. Those years teaching provided her with valuable insight into the parent-child dynamic.

This insightful book is a wonderful guide for all parents who want to steer their children to be the best they can be.

—Linda Grice Lynch, parent, artist, animator, and sculptor

Endorsements

In the past fifty years, I have spent much of my time in teaching parents to understand and enjoy their children. My daughter, Marita, has grown up with these valuable principles and has substantially added to the body of work on the topic. We are both pleased that Edwina Neely has incorporated the concepts of the personalities from our work along with her vivid illustrations and fresh insights. It is our hope that as you read *Children Are Gifts*, you will discover the uniqueness and giftedness of the personalities of each of your children and that you will love them in a new way. Once you see the importance of this understanding in raising your children, as Edwina has done, you'll be passing it on to other parents as well.

—Florence Littauer, author of the best-selling book *Personality Plus,* and Marita Littauer, author of *Wired That Way*

"Telling stories of your and your husband's childhood is compelling and relatable.

Stories about your children reveal that this is not just a book of words but a real-life love story."

If you are reading this book because parenting with excellence is vitally important to you, please enjoy learning from the best!

I met Edwina Neely over thirty years ago when she was honing her amazing skills as a volunteer teacher. Her love for children, all children, is infectious. When she says, "We should view each child as a book, not to be written, but to be read," you will learn not just why this principle must guide our child-parent relationships but simple ways you can do it too.

Edwina Neely's lifetime work is cherishing children and their giftedness. Personal stories from her own family as well as hundreds of practical examples she's created from professional experiences will amaze and inspire you. Her methods work. Consider this book her gift to you.

—Debra Brill, parent and vice president of Seventh-day Adventist Church, North American Division

For almost twenty years, Edwina and I have shared the joy of working with children as teachers, as well as children ministries certified presenters. Edwina is absolutely passionate about helping parents to motivate their children to use and develop their God-given gifts to reach their highest potential. In fact, as a teacher, she influenced the lives of my children, grown-ups now, instilling in them a positive attitude of self-confidence that remains today.

Children Are Gifts is a remarkable book, written skillfully with a mix of professional expertise and practical wisdom coming from her long and vast daily life experiences.

As a parent, grandparent, educator, and professional counselor, I found this book to be a must-have guide for parents, as well as for anyone invested in raising gifted, happy, responsible, and successful children.

—Carmen Esposito, parent, educator, and professional counselor in psychology

I first met Edwina as she was starting her last year teaching kindergarten full time. We met walking, and over hundreds if not thousands of walks, I have listened with great interest and respect to her thoughts, feelings, and beliefs on parenting and teaching. We always stop to say hello to the young people we meet as we walk since that is where her heart and soul are. Reading this book, I realize most of its content I have discussed with her. As a parent of two who have now flown the nest, and as a registered dietitian who has worked with families over the last forty-plus years, I heartily endorse the wisdom of her philosophy toward parenting. In this book I see the great joy Edwina takes in parenting and her understanding of the uniqueness of each individual. The world is a better place for her efforts to support parents and enhance the lives of the youngest and very fortunate that she does not retire but continues to teach parenting.

—Margaret McLellan, parent, MS RD

Edwina's joy for life and passion for helping parents raise good children emanates from her person, and she has captured this so well in the book you are about to read. She loved raising her own children and teaching others, and her many years of experience have resulted in a great wisdom about how to love and lead children to growth in maturity and a confidence in themselves. Her joy and wisdom, combined with her deep Christian faith, make her an excellent resource for parents in the thick of child-rearing, like myself. As a mother to six young children, I am inspired by Edwina's encouragement to love these children tenderly, to enjoy them, and to lead them confidently, with unwavering respect for their individuality. Our children are gifts to be cherished, and the book in your hands will remind you of that while giving you concrete ways to help you unwrap, understand, and enjoy these gifts from God.

—Meredith Daniel, parent and home school teacher

This book is all about unpacking the gifts that lay within your child—unveiling the genius within. It provides useful tips for parents with children of all ages. I found the chapters "How We Learn: Five Gifts" and "The Way They Should Go: Parts 1 and 2—Unique Gifts and Understanding Temperaments" eye opening. Although my children are in elementary and middle school, this book provided hands-on, real-life examples of how I can communicate with and better understand my children. As a Christian, this book continually reminded me that my children are gifts from God to be cherished and understood. As a parent, it is comforting to know that through God's guidance, in connection with the tools in this book, I can strive to be the best parent God wants me to be.

—Ava Wilt, parent and human resources manager

More than ever in our increasingly secularized world, children desperately need to know that they are loved and esteemed by their parents and significant loved ones. This impacts the lives of our little ones as they develop a deep sense of trust and security.

Edwina's parenting workshops have significantly enhanced parents' skills and supported them with raising gifted spiritual champions in the home. The topic of one of her cherished presentations was entitled "Children Are Gifts from God." Parents were enlightened by Edwina's unique way of conveying the uniqueness of each child.

As director of a children's ministry, I have developed a heartfelt appreciation for Edwina's gift of communication. She lovingly interacts with others to provide attainable strategies for the development of stronger families.

Don't miss reading this amazing book! It will be a valuable resource for teachers, parents, and anyone who ministers to children. This is especially relevant for young parents. Each chapter contains helpful information supported by a godly perspective. Moreover, you'll be inspired and equipped to view children as the gifts from God.

—Michael Edward Franklin, parent and director of children's ministry

No one could be better prepared than Edwina Neely to write a book on positive parenting. Edwina has not only spent her life teaching and training other people's children, but she and her husband, Bill, have also raised a competent and loving family of their own. I have known Edwina for probably more years than either of us care to admit to, and never have I known her to be other than a committed wife and mother. No matter how many other jobs she may have had, family came first. I remember visiting her one time when she was expecting her last child. She told me how important it was for her and Bill to talk directly to their unborn child. After the baby's birth, I visited again. After "oohing" and "aahing" over Priska, she showed me how the baby tried to follow the sound of her and Bill's voices. That made me a believer in her knowledge of even the yet-to-be-born child. Those who read this book and put into practice what they read will be much blessed. Thank you, Edwina, for sharing your knowledge and secrets of child raising. You have been a blessing in my life.

—Barbara Manspeaker, parent and children's ministries director

Children Are Gifts

A PARENT'S GUIDE TO
Raising Gifted, Confident, Happy Children

Edwina Grice Neely

WESTBOW
PRESS®
A DIVISION OF THOMAS NELSON
& ZONDERVAN

WestBow Press books may be ordered through booksellers or by contacting:

WestBow Press
A Division of Thomas Nelson & Zondervan
1663 Liberty Drive
Bloomington, IN 47403
www.westbowpress.com
1 (866) 928-1240

ISBN: 978-1-9736-2400-4 (sc)
ISBN: 978-1-9736-2402-8 (hc)
ISBN: 978-1-9736-2401-1 (e)

Library of Congress Control Number: 2018903750

Print information available on the last page.

WestBow Press rev. date: 04/23/2018

This book is dedicated to

my husband, Bill;

my late son, B.G., who always encouraged me to do great things;

my daughters, Nicole, Lakisha, and Priska;

and my sister, Linda.

Contents

Foreword

This book will open your eyes and open your heart
to the unspoken needs of your children.

We all love children, but as a mother, I didn't always understand mine. Sometimes it seemed too bad that one size didn't fit all. No, I'm not talking about clothes. I'm speaking of how I parented and how my children responded. And that's the reason I'm excited about this book.

Each of our four was dearly loved, but still things didn't always go smoothly. It was almost as if each had their own language, and in a way, they did. As Neely explains, each of us has our own unique gifts and temperament. Understanding and working with, instead of against, your child's temperament will make a great difference in the happiness you will experience as a family.

This deeply spiritual guide provides practical help so that both moms and dads can be the parents God designed them to be. Chapter titles such as "Free to Be Me (Be the Parent God Made You to Be)," "I Am What You Call Me," and "Joys in Listening: Positive Communication" will lay a foundation for your happy, loving, and disciplined home.

This book is a must read for caring parents.

Penny Estes Wheeler

writer and editor

Preface

It is not an accident that you have this book in your hands. You are aware of the important role we have as parents, and you want to know more. This book is designed to be a guidebook for parents. It is intended to encourage you along your parenting journey as well as give you creative ideas to make parenting fun and rewarding. You're invited to go with me on a journey to consider ways to raise gifted, confident, happy children through everyday experiences.

This book was written to bring back to parents' consciousness the important role we have as parents. I am making a plea that parents be parents again and stop letting the media and strangers teach our children. We as parents have the opportunity and privilege to nurture the wonderful gifts God has rewarded us with—our children! We have been chosen by God to be parents, and we have a divine responsibility to train our children to be what God intended them to be.

In this book I review our role as parents, explain how serious our job is, and give ideas we can use to develop our children to be kind, loving, responsible citizens.

I want parents to see the need to create a learning environment in their homes that meets each child's needs. It's a fun job and an awesome responsibility when we see that everything we do is teaching. This book shows how learning can be fun. It helps parents see that they don't have to entertain their children to have quality time with them. *Wherever* we are and *whatever* we are doing with our children is a *teaching moment.*

You will see that family is important and each person in the family has a role to play. We all connect and should sense that we all belong and have an important role in our society.

Relax, and realize you can teach math, science, and Bible without sitting down to read a book or playing a game with your child. Don't get me wrong—reading to your child is very important. If your day has gone by and you have to choose one thing to do with your child—read!

As you read this book, you will develop concrete ideas you can do at home with your child and still get your work done. Help your child learn every moment of every day as you enjoy life together.

Every day you have the opportunity to lead your child to the source of all understanding, meaning, wonderment, knowledge, and wisdom of God. You can show your children the God of the water you bathe them in, the God of the food you feed them, the God of the home they live in, the God of nature, family, and friends, and the only God to worship.

You will discover concrete, practical, and creative ways to teach many concepts to raise your gifted child; gain insights on how children learn, their temperaments and personalities, modes of learning, spiritual gifts, and unique giftedness; and experience the joys of parenting: in listening and effective communication, in disciple with love, in family worship, in the bathroom, in the kitchen, and outdoors.

This is more than a book: consider it to be a tool that you can use anytime, anywhere. You can carry it with you when you are in the doctor's office or in line in the grocery store. This tool can help you make use of every teachable moment. Simply take it out and get a new idea of an activity you can do with your child as well as read an encouraging word to help on your journey.

So I invite you to journey with me and discover the joy of parenting.

Acknowledgments

I want to thank:

Lakisha, for reading my book in the roughest form
and taking time to write comments for me to improve
when I first started writing my book years ago.

Vikki Montgomery, for getting me started to get my book published.

Linda, for encouraging me from the West Coast.

Margaret, my walking buddy, for listening to me ramble on
about my concerns for parents while we walked for hours.

Priska, for editing some chapters for me even with your busy schedule.

Ava, for reading my book when I first started years
ago, reading it again, and endorsing it.

Carmen, my buddy and team teacher.

Debra Brill, for wisdom on the direction of my book.

Nicole for being my photographer and graphic designer.

Meredith Daniel, for being my faithful supporter.

I also thank:

Florence Littauer, a best-selling writer, who inspired me to present seminars on "personalities" and endorsed my book.

Michael Franklin, supporter of my parents' ministry.

Barbara, supporter of my children's ministry.

Parents that encouraged me to write this book.

Parents who entrusted me with their children these forty-plus years of teaching.

Finally, I thank God for prompting me to write this book and giving me the strength and determination to complete it.

May this book be a blessing to all!

Introduction

Mother's Dilemma

I gave up my career as a speech pathologist to be at home with my son. One morning I lay wondering, "This baby is only seven months old. I have four years and five months left before he will be old enough to go to kindergarten. What am I to do with him? What?"

This may be the feeling of other at-home mothers or fathers. Some of the special feelings of having a newborn baby have worn off, and feelings of loneliness, helplessness, and worry have set in. Even wonderment— "I can bathe the baby, keep him clean, play with him, feed him, and give him something to drink. I can clean the house, cook the meals, wash the clothes—is this my job description for the next four years? Heaven help me! I'm tired of this routine already!" Yes, this was my job description.

Yes, this is your job description, yet the joy is found between the lines. You have chosen one of the most important jobs of a lifetime, one you will never regret when you concentrate on the joys between the lines.

Dilemma Settled

Fortunately, I was not alone. My most amazing husband was willing to do anything that needed to be done. His dad died when he was six years old, and his mother taught him how to cook, how to sew, how to do laundry, how to clean floors, how to braid his sister's hair, and the list goes on. He could do so much I did wonder some days why he needed me. After children, it was clear; God had given me an awesome man with the potential to be a great helper. So when the baby's diaper needed to be changed, he helped with that, when my daughter's hair needed to be braided, he helped with that, and when the clothes needed to be washed, he did it. He'd always say, "I did it because it needed to be done." I really believed he did it to show his love for me. He didn't see men and women as having different roles. We were partners and worked together doing whatever needed to be done at the time.

I am thankful to God for my husband. He has been a tremendous father and husband over these forty-eight years. We are partners and have chosen one of the most important jobs of a lifetime: being parents!

Sketch of Life's Journey

I spent fourteen years at home with my children. These fourteen years could have been prison, misery, and unhappiness, but thanks be to God, they were very profitable years for me and my family. I am not saying I never had down-times; I did. However, overall I see those years as a blessing. God has taught me so much through my career as a mother, and I want to share it with others.

The idea to write this book came to me one morning in North Carolina, during my morning devotions. God gave me a view of the whole book, including the introduction and table of contents. I knew I had to begin writing. I did begin to write. However, life happens. Being a parent of three children now, my main job was being the best parent I could be. So my writing was sporadic.

I did not like the idea of leaving my children with a babysitter, so I considered other options. Since I had a master's in speech pathology, I just had to take a few courses, and I qualified to have a certified preschool/daycare in my home. It was called Loving Angels Daycare. For fourteen years I could teach my children at home and have an income. Most of all

I was happy to be at home with my children to instill in them my values. I could teach them about God every day.

My two-year-old could recite the twenty-third Psalm perfectly. The children learned how to recite the books of the Bible and many Bible verses. I taught Bible, science, math, reading, and spelling with a song. I later developed a seminar called "Teach It with a Song" and had the honor of presenting at a national teachers' convention one year. I began creating seminars on how to make bread with children. I became a certified presenter for the daycare association and had the privilege of teaching other daycare providers. These years developed foundational chapters for my book. I had fourteen years of experience at home.

When I started working outside of the home, I taught in the elementary schools. My passion to help parents continued, and for many years now, I have been a seminar presenter and traveled internationally, sharing my ideas with teachers and parents.

Years have passed, and our journey as parents has been an incredible one. When we married, we were young, both twenty-three. We knew we wanted to be parents. I wanted twelve children, and then I went down to six. I had four and I thank God for what each one taught me. We always knew we wanted to be the best parents we could be. We immediately read books on parenting and went to parenting seminars, even becoming certified in presenting parenting seminars. The joy of parenting is our theme. It has been a joy no words can explain.

When our first child was born, Bill's job required him to travel a lot. This meant he had to be away from his family. I remember one night when I picked him up from a long trip, something happened that changed his life. In those days we held our children in our arms while someone else did the driving. Bill was holding our son. As he lifted him up in the air, he noticed his son was looking at him in a puzzled way. Bill said, in his mind, he could hear his son saying, "I know I've seen this man some place before." *My son doesn't know who I am!* were Bill's thoughts. This incident had such a profound effect on Bill that he got another job so he would not have to be away from his family. We took parenting seriously. We are grateful to have been blessed with four children—one son and three daughters.

I urge parents to enjoy your children while you can. Let's thank God for each moment we have with our children.

Whether you're a stay-at-home mom or stay-at-home dad, or a parent who works outside the home, that's okay because this book is for those of you who want to be the best mom or dad you can be during the time you are with your child. This book is designed to provide incredible ideas you can do at home and principles that can be extended anywhere you are with your child.

Wherever and whenever you are with your child, make it quality time. The time you spend with your family is determining the quality of your family and the influence you have on their future.

Thanks for joining me as you raise gifted, confident, and happy children!

PART 1

Encouraging Parents:
Understanding Parents' Role
in Raising Gifted, Confident,
and Happy Children

PART I

CHAPTER 1

Children: Gifts from God

You have been blessed with a gift from God just as you are a gift from God to your parents. If this is a new thought for you, I want you to stop now and say, "I am a gift from God!" Believe it, and from this day forward, think of your child as a gift just as you are a gift. You see, no matter how you or your child got here, how you or your child looks, or which abilities you or your child possess, we're all gifts from God (Psalm 127:3 NCV). No child is a mistake or accident. Psalm 127 also tells us that children are rewards from God. You have found favor with God, and He has rewarded you with this little bundle of life. Remember there is no one else on earth like your little one. You can look the whole world over, and there is no one like your baby. When God made your baby, He threw away the mold and the template, and you can't scan it back in and make another. God never prefabs or mass produces people. Tell your child, "You're the only you God made."

This child, your reward, has been gifted with unique abilities. As parents we are to study our children and allow God to show us how they are gifted and train them up (Proverbs 22:6 NIV) in that way. In the original Hebrew Bible we learn *way* means "the natural proclivity or natural bent of the child." "How is your child gifted?" is the question. Study your child's behaviors, interests, likes and dislikes, and preferences and abilities. It takes time, patience, unconditional love, and daily observation. Find the answers to these questions about your child:

- What is your child good at?
- What interests him or her the most?
- How does she or he learn?
- What does she or he like to talk about?
- What does she or he like to do?
- What makes her or him tick?
- How does your child play with siblings and friends?
- Is she or he a leader or a follower?

Now, answer the following questions about yourself:

- What do we like to do together?
- Do I talk more than I listen to my child?
- How do I communicate with my child?
- Do I allow my child to do what he or she is capable of doing?
- Do I use my words to heal rather than hurt?
- Do I need to work on my patience?
- Do I accept my child's personality, or would I like to change it?

"The greatest gift you can give your child is not your riches, but helping your child discover his or her giftedness."

Joseph Chilton Pearce, author of the book *Magical Child and the Crack in the Cosmic Egg*, writes,

"What we must provide is an appropriate environment, which means one rich with concrete experience and offering complete emotional security for the child, free of threat. Within the first three years of life the absorbent mind of the child has either opened up to embrace a benevolent universe or closed down into a frightened defense mechanism on guard against a world it can't 'trust'."

God has provided your child with everything he or she needs for success. As parents we play a critical role in the lives of our children. Our children learn to trust us when we are consistent in our love and teachings. The mother and father are the first and most important models in a child's life. It is clear to me that the beginning years of our children's lives are crucial.

If you are a stay-at-home parent, it would prove to be an investment worth making. If you take your child to a caregiver, be a tenacious detective in deciding whom you will trust with your precious gift. Recognizing your child as a gift from God is the first step of the journey.

CHAPTER 2

Parents: Called by God

Parenting is the most important job on earth. Every person on earth comes from parents. What happens the first three to five years of your child's life is vital. Remember, you are the most important person in the life of your child.

You have the opportunity to develop values, beliefs, traditions, life skills, experiences, and knowledge. This foundation will stay with your child for the rest of his or her life. When God made this world, He said, "Be fruitful and multiply" (Genesis 1:28 KJV). You have been called by God to be a parent. Thank God for making you a parent!

Moms and dads were given the ability to join together and produce a child. The mother was given a special place for your little gift to grow while she or he is being formed by God. The mother is blessed by God to participate in the development of a child. Psalm 139:13 (NCV) says, "You made my whole being; you formed me in my mother's body."

You delivered this child into this world, and you, with God, participated in the physical birth. Even if your child is adopted or a stepchild, God has entrusted this child into your hands, and you have the opportunity to participate in your child's spiritual birth. Moms and dads have been given the responsibility to nurture, teach, protect, and love this special gift they have been given.

You are with your child every day, and everything you do teaches your child about God or about something in God's world. You are giving your child a spiritual foundation that will remain with him or her all of his or her life. God has gifted your child. As parents we have to study our children and watch their giftedness be revealed. This theme recurs throughout this book.

Every day *you* have the opportunity to lead your children to the source of all understanding, meaning, wonderment, knowledge, and wisdom—God. You can show your children the God of the water you bathe them in, the God of food you feed them, the God of the home they live in, the God of nature, family, and friends, the God who deserves our worship.

As your child grows daily, you will see human nature form. You will see behaviors that surprise you. At about six months old your child can control the household if you let it happen. We must remember we are the parents, and that means God has given us the authority and permission to tell our children what to do, to not negotiate with our children, to not make deals with our children, and to not threaten or bribe our children. You want your child to see that you are put here by God to protect, love, and guide him or her to grow up to be a wonderful, obedient, happy, well-disciplined child. You are here to help him or her become a helpful member of society, to make this world a better place.

Consider this profound statement by Joseph Chilton Pearce: "What we are teaches the child far more than what we say, so we must be what we want our children to become." As parents we must examine ourselves and determine if we are being who we want our children to be.

You are here to teach and train your child in the way your child should go. Proverbs 22:6 (KJV) says, "Train up a child in the way he should go: and when he is old, he will not depart from it." Remember, in this text the word *way* means "the natural proclivity, the bent of your child." We have to train them up in their natural way, and they will not depart from it. Is that a new thought for you? Each child comes with different personalities, talents, spiritual gifts, and abilities, and as parents we have the big job of helping our children to love God, themselves, and others.

Let's take a moment and consider this illustration: Think of a seed. That seed has the potential to become a tree producing an abundance of fruit. Now think of your child as a seed. Your child has great potential. Like the seed, he or she needs attention, nurturing, and training to flourish. Could you put the tree in the seed? That's absurd, right? But that is what we are doing when we try to make our children what we want them to be rather than allowing their God-given potential be revealed. Yes! I know many times we want to force our unattained dreams upon our children. However, if we force our children to become doctors or lawyers when those are not their gifts, then we have unhappy people doing something they hate. I have heard many people say their parents wanted them to be a doctor, a lawyer, or a pastor, and they went to school to study in those fields. However, today they are doing what they love and not what they studied in college. It is not worth the effort, hard work, or money trying to make our children become what we want them to be.

You participate in your child's physical and spiritual development in a powerful way, guiding him or her to be the child God made him or her to be. Tell yourself, "I am important in my child's life. I am a parent!"

CHAPTER 3

Be the Parent God Made You to Be

God wants you to be the best parent you can be. Every child is unique, and there are many ways of parenting. But there is an approach to raising children that produces healthy, mature adults.

Because you and your spouse may have experienced different parenting styles, it is imperative that you work together on deciding how you want to raise your child. According to Victorious Christian Living International, Inc. there are four types of parenting styles: effective, neglectful, controlling, and permissive.

The effective parenting style speaks for itself. Naturally we would choose to be effective parents. This style of parenting utilizes both high acceptance and high accountability techniques. I believe the effective style is the best style of parenting. Most of us are working to be effective parents.

Let's evaluate the other three parenting styles, determine if there are any similarities with your parenting style, and decide what aspects need to be removed to be an effective parent.

The permissive parent exercises high levels of acceptance but low levels of accountability.

Permissive parenting is characterized by *undercorrection*, that is, there is little attempt by a parent to control the actions of one's child. The parent may attempt to correct the child but gives up if that attempt fails. They allow their child's disobedience to continue.

You have seen this parent in the store. The child wants something. The parent says, "No you can't get it." The child has a temper tantrum. The child gets the candy. Who is in control—the parent or the child?

The *effective parent* would talk to the child before going to the store, and the child would know beforehand what he or she can get or what's not permissible. If the child asks for something that is not permissible, the effective parent simply reminds the child of their agreement. The child might test the parent to see if he or she really means what he or she says, but the effective parent remains in control, and the child can do nothing to change the parent's mind.

The neglectful parent has low acceptance *with* low accountability.

Neglectful parenting is characterized by absence, spending a little time with the child and/or some forms of abandonment. When a mother or father is absent, the parent cannot give either acceptance or accountability. No matter what the parent's affections may be, the reality to the child is abandonment. The neglectful parent may have an excuse for his absence citing having to work to provide for the child. However, the child will feel uncared for and unimportant.

Controlling parents have low acceptance *with* high accountability.

Controlling parenting is characterized *overcorrecting, belittling, criticizing,* or being *over-protective.*

You have seen parents who are harsh and inflexible. These parents might ridicule or ignore the child. They are always reminding the child of past failures. These parents could be abusive. They use fear to get the child to obey and are mean and scream at their children. Children of these parents usually have low self-esteem because they have received so many put-downs.

I believe that the effective style of parenting is best approach to raising children that produces healthy, mature adults, and each of us should be working to be effective parents. I recognize that each personality has a design by God and that each of us is unique and this will impact the way we parent. Because you are you, your parenting style will be different. There's no need to compare yourself with others. However, you may want to consider how you and your spouse will integrate your unique personalities and beliefs with what you know to be traits of effective parenting. One suggestion is to reminisce on your parents' parenting styles and determine whether you would like to adopt their style or develop one of your own. You should also develop a parenting plan whereby you and your spouse take time to communicate how you will intentionally and purposefully parent.

My husband and I had to sit down and discuss our parenting styles. He came from a single-parent home. When he was six, his father died, and he then became the man of the house. His mother was a very controlling parent and was physically abusive and used cutting words that damaged. He doesn't remember hearing his mother say, "I love you," during his childhood. His mother would ridicule and condemn him. He never felt he could please her.

He said he lived in fear that she would kill him because she would always say, "Boy, don't you know I will kill you?"

He got yelled at for everything he said or did. He felt emotionally wounded and rejected. I am sharing this much detail because whoever is reading this, I want you to know that the type of parenting style that children live with influences their whole lives, including their marriage. It took years before my husband could accept that I loved him unconditionally no matter what. He never felt accepted, so it was difficult for him to believe I could accept him.

I feel I was chosen to marry him to bring love into his life and a sense of worth. As parents much of what we do become life commandments. We have the power to determine our child's destiny.

Thankfully we decided we did not want to be controlling parents. My parents' parenting style was one sided. My dad would say, "Do whatever you mother tells you." He may have been at home but neglected to be involved in our lives. My mother was very affirming, and I would say she was an effective parent. My two siblings and I felt accepted, and we were taught accountability.

I think one of the most important things about parenting is what you say and how you say it. Deciding on your parenting style is a very important decision. To *be effective parents, both* of you have to agree. When your child sees Mom and Dad are not together on how to discipline, they will choose sides and say, "But Mom said," or "Dad said."

It does take time to sit down with your mate and decide what you both will agree on. However, it is so very important. Your child or children can have consistency in their lives and will feel loved and cared for. Talk about what you expect them to do (when they are eating, when it's bedtime, during bathtime, etc.) Talk about your method of discipline. (Will you spank or use timeouts? Decide on consequences.)

If there is no spouse, it is important to talk to the other caregiver (daycare provider, grandma, mom, or whoever will be sharing in this parenting journey). Agree on the type of parenting style you choose. My husband and I decided to strive to be effective parents and work toward that goal. When both parents strive to be effective parents, you will find peace in your household. As days go by and as your child grows older, you will have to make changes, adjustments, and modifications to meet the present need. Striving to be effective parents takes patience with yourself and with your child.

Remember the scripture: "I can do all things through Christ, because he gives me strength" (Philippians 4:13 NCV). You are not alone!

I want to reiterate the importance of consistent parenting in parents or any caregiver that will be involved with your child. Having the same parenting style makes the child feel secure and loved.

I have seen children who have a joint custody situation and the environment is so different the child becomes confused and many times disruptive behavior is manifest at home or in school. You hear about children having emotional problems. Many times it stems from the home environment. Be confident and consistent in your parenting style.

Striving to be effective parents is a journey.

As our children grow and get older, our parenting changes to meet the needs of the child at that moment. When our children are small, we are teaching them boundaries, expectations, limitations, responsibilities, and life skills, such as manners, being respectful, and much more. When your child is a teenager, you shouldn't have to tell him or her when to say thank you or pick up his or her clothes off of the floor. When children know what to expect, they feel confident and will happily carry out what's expected because they know it pleases you. I warn you, though, there will be times when your child will test you to see if you really mean what you say. They want to know if they can *trust* you. Are you a keeper of your word? You have heard, "Say what you mean and mean what you say." That is important.

Now we know children will be children, and sometimes they will make up something to keep from telling the truth. I can't remember who told this story. One day I heard a story told about a parent who was talking to his child about wetting the bed. I don't know the name of the person who told this story. This is how the story goes. The child said a cat did it. The father explained that they had a tiny kitten and the bed had a big wet circle in it. The child then said, "The window was open and a *big cat* came through the window and wet on her bed." The father knew she was making up this story, but he just had her to change her sheets and accepted the story.

A few days later she came to her dad and told the truth. Our children really want to please us, and when we keep from getting upset and screaming and telling children they are lying and start putting them down, telling them how bad they are, the outcome can be similar—a confession in their own time. The child knew she was lying, and she felt safe enough to tell her dad the truth without being condemned. She knew she was still loved.

I'm reminded of another story that happened when my son was in high school. The team was getting expensive tennis shoes, and he wanted a pair. He knew we couldn't afford the shoes, but he just begged to get them.

Trying to make us feel bad, he said, "Mom, Dad, everybody's getting them. Please can I?"

In a calm tone, we continued to say *no*. A few weeks later he came to us and said, "I really didn't want those shoes. I just wanted to see if you would get them." Sometimes they just want to see if we stick to our word. If they know how many times they can ask before you give in, you have programmed them that way.

Be careful. Our children are very smart. They know how to push your hot button and get what they want. We have to be strong and *stick to our word*! We can change our mind about a situation, but be sure to make it clear that *you* decided and it was not because your child nagged you. Or it can be a negotiation. Here's an example for older children: if it's a movie they want to go to and you don't approve of their choice of movie, you can give them choices of movies you approve to pick from. You are still in control, and they can be happy and get to go to a movie. Pleading and begging for the other movie they wanted is not allowed.

Remember, children are masters at manipulation. Let's look at this scenario with a younger child. Here the child is testing and seeking trust.

Just let's say the rule is, "You can get dessert when you eat your dinner."

The child knows this very well. But look at what can happen. The child does not finish his dinner; basically, he just played in his food. Later Mother is cleaning up the kitchen and he comes in the kitchen saying, "Mommy, you're the bestest mommy in the world. I love you. Can I have a cookie?"

Now, Mommy can go into preaching mode, raising her voice and telling the child the rule and fussing at him for asking. Or she could say, "Yes, when you finish your dinner tomorrow."

Or she could say in her mind, "He's such a good boy I'll just let him have a cookie even though he didn't finish his dinner."

Now the first response was putting down and yelling. Not very effective! The second response is using a positive approach, knowing the child knows the rule, and passing the test. Yes, this is just a test. In the last response, the parent failed the test. The child may have been happy to get the cookie, but deep down within he's thinking, "I can't even trust them over a little cookie." The child will wonder if he can get away with this again or if he can get Mommy to change her mind if he just butters her up with a little praise. When the mother kept her word and told the child *when* he could have a cookie, he may not have appeared to be happy, but he was learning the important fact: "Mommy keeps her word."

Understanding that we are *the parents* and we need to *keep our word* is imperative in raising gifted, competent, and happy children. It is a challenge to be an effective parent.

We can all strive to be effective parents, loving our children unconditionally as God loves us!

Ephesians 6:4 (KJV) reminds us of how important it is to keep from making our children angry. It says, "Fathers, do not make your children angry, but raise them with the training and teaching of the Lord." This text is applicable to all parents. We should not make unreasonable demands, showing favoritism or humiliating our children. God's unconditional love should shine through.

Our challenge is to be consistent and obedient to God's Word. Remember, we are not alone. In Matthew 28:20 (KJV) Jesus says, "I am with you always, even unto the end of the world."

CHAPTER 4

How We Learn: Five Gifts

God has given us five gifts to learn—the five senses.

We have the sense of sight or visual sense, the sense of hearing or auditory sense, the sense of smell or olfactory sense, the sense of touch or tactile/kinesthetic sense, and the sense of taste or gustatory sense. These senses are called modes of learning or learning styles. In the brain we have certain modalities, and each sense represents a mode of learning.

Your newborn baby is ready to explore all these wonderful senses.

All information is received through one of these avenues. You will notice your baby is fascinated with the sense of touch, and everything goes to the mouth. That's okay. Just be sure your baby puts things that are safe in the mouth. (Just a little motherly advice.)

Deborah McNelis in her writing called *Brain Insights* explains what the baby feels. She states this as if the baby is talking: "Repeated tender caring makes strong connections in my brain telling me that I am worthwhile and cared about. Knowing I am loved is the most important thing I need to learn as an infant."

Even though we have been given these gifts, we usually favor one of them. So as you observe your child, you will soon notice what he or she prefers. You have heard people say, "I have to see it to get it" (visual). Or "Just tell me. I'll remember" (auditory). Or "Will you show me how to do this?" (Tactile-kinesthetic).

Each one of these statements is telling you something about the sense that is preferred. If your child wants to see it or you observe him or her looking closely at things or he or she prefers seeing the book instead of just hearing you read, your child is probably a visual learner. This child likes to see things or prefers to use the sense of sight to learn. Avoid making a hasty decision because your child is just beginning to explore and develop a favorite sense. Children who like to hear music or listen to someone reading a book or who can carry out a direction with just a verbal command are auditory learners. They like to hear things or prefer to learn by using the auditory mode of learning.

Right now as you enjoy your precious gift from God, provide experiences using all of the senses. Talk, talk, talk to your baby. Speech is learned, and the more you talk, the more intelligent your baby will become. Let your baby feel various textures: a soft stuffed animal, a rough kiwi, a smooth apple, a rubbery orange, cold water, warm water, a soft cotton ball, a round cherry, and a long carrot. Notice all of the things around you are a teaching tool. While you show the items, *be sure to talk about each thing. Remember, talking is the key.*

When you are nursing your baby or bottle feeding your baby, talk to the baby about the tasty, warm milk he or she is drinking. When your baby begins eating solid food, talk about the color of the food, the texture of the food, and the taste of the food.

When you bathe and dress the baby, talk about the parts of the body while in the water. Look in the mirror and let the baby see his or her body. *Thank You God for My Body* will be a useful book for teaching the body parts. In this book children learn to be thankful using a cute little rhyme. For example, to teach about eyes, the rhyme says: "Thank you God for eyes to see the pretty world you made for me."

Teach your baby what things are to touch, what things are to just look at, and what things are to taste, smell, and hear. Everything will fascinate your baby. You may find him or her just staring at a light for minutes, or your baby may want to suck a finger or chew on his toes. Every child is unique. Accept your baby just as he or she is.

When you are home with your baby, you have the opportunity to take him or her with you everywhere you go and in every room you have teaching tools. As parents we have the opportunity to develop each sense to the max, and one day your little one will reveal to you his or her favorite sense, and you will know the preferred mode of learning. We must be diligent to attend and listen to the sensory modes of expression our children are exhibiting. When we know how they learn best, we can provide them with the greatest joy of learning and living.

I want to share with you a story of an experience from childhood that will help you understand what I mean by listening to your child and how he or she expresses his or her favorite mode of learning.

I was nine years old. One day I was going shopping with my mother. My mother parked the car. I stood watching as she filled the meter with coins. I saw each coin go into the meter. We were going shopping, and I knew the meter would need to be filled again soon. And I would be the one to do it. I stayed close to Mom as we walked down the street. I wanted to make sure I didn't get lost from her. Sure enough, the time ran out, and Mom gave me money to go feed the meter. Which way do I go? I had forgotten. I didn't even notice the way we walked. Tears ran down my face. Feelings of inadequacy flooded my mind. *You should know the way. You forgot! You didn't notice!* my brain screamed.

When I returned to Mom with wet coins in my hands from holding them so tightly, I had to say, "I forgot where the car was."

You dummy. You forgot, I thought. My mother never said those words. She'd say, "Oh Edwina!" I guess I could hear it in her tone.

Just recently fifty-nine years later, I questioned why those words "you forgot" brought feeling of rage. As a teacher the students would occasionally say, "Teacher, you forgot …" I would get so angry and wondered why. *What's making me so angry?*

Then I went back to my childhood shopping days and relived the experiences.

I am very visual and need visual reinforcement to remember. She wasn't listening!

Our children are telling us who they are, but we must listen and attend,

Listen to the way they live, talk, learn, and play. How do they use their five senses? All I needed was *visual prompts* as we walked, and I would have remembered where the car was parked.

We all have five modes of learning, but we prefer certain ones. I am very visual. If my mom was listening, she would have known I remembered things I *see*. I am grateful for my mother, for she did observe me and *realized* I was a visual learner and provided me with visual stimulation. Today I can help other parents.

As you observe your child, you will know what sense your child needs to learn and what mode of learning he or she prefers.

I'm reminded of another story of a child I had in kindergarten. As you observe your child, you will know what sense your child needs to learn, but this story helps us see the importance of finding the mode of learning your child needs to learn.

Rosemarie was already six, and she was in kindergarten a second time. Her previous teacher held her back. Rosemarie's mother was really concerned, saying, "This is her second year in kindergarten, and she still can't remember her alphabet!" I listened to her concern and immediately started looking for ways to help her learn her alphabet. She had memorized the sequence and was able to say what letter came before and after each other. For example, I could point to a letter and ask, "What letter is this?" If I said, "It's after g," she would say, "H." She had just memorized the names of the letters, but she could not visually recognize the letters and give the correct name. I noticed Rosemarie liked to hug and be close to people, so I decided to try a tactile/kinesthetic approach. She always missed all of her spelling words even though she could copy them beautifully. I gave her some clay one day and said, "Rosemarie, we are going to spell the words using clay today." She was excited because she was able to make beautiful creations out of clay. After she formed the letters to spell the words, I had her feel the letters and then name the sounds of the letters. She spelled all of her words correctly that week and many more to come.

By the end of the year, she knew all of the alphabet and the letter sounds and was on her way to reading. Rosemarie needed to use her tactile/kinesthetic sense. I was able to identify her mode of learning. That was her strength, and learning happened.

Being aware of the sensory words we use is very beneficial when we talk.

We must be careful about how we talk. When we talk us use words such as "see that" (visual), "listen to this" (auditory), or "feel this" (tactile-kinesthetic), oftentimes we are speaking in a different sensory language. The child may be saying, "Show me" (visual), and we respond by saying, "Didn't you hear me?" (auditory), rather than saying, "Look at it this way" (visual—responding in their mode). Or a child might say, "I need to hear that again" (auditory). And we say, "Don't you see this?" answering in the visual mode. Another example is when a child might say, "I don't feel it" (tactile/kinesthetic), and we respond and say, "Look at this" (visual) rather than saying, "Touch this or would you like to do it."

When you start noticing what sensory mode you prefer, you can enjoy the discovery of your child's mode. The job of the parent is to listen, attend, observe our children, and determine your children's favorite sensory mode of learning.

God has given us five gifts, but all of us have a favorite. Teach your child using all five senses so your child can receive maximum learning.

The following is example to teach your child through the visual and auditory sense. Imagine it is spring in Maryland. If you live somewhere where the seasons do not change, just imagine. In Maryland spring is announced with a bright bushy yellow plant called forsythia. Look at all the things this bush can teach. The forsythia bush has four petals on each flower. The petals have points on each end. This bush, like magic, turns green quickly. It does not matter how big this bush gets; it'll always be a bush and not a tree. Conversation could include: "Look at the forsythia! The forsythia is yellow. The forsythia has four petals. Let's count them— one, two, three, and four. Look at the points on each petal. Four points. The forsythia is a bush. God made the pretty forsythia."

Here you are repeating forsythia many times because repetition is important for learning to take place. You are teaching shapes, color, counting, and identifying the bush, and you are drawing to their minds the creator of the bush. Whatever you are showing your baby, talk, talk, talk, and share all of the information you can think of.

You are your child's first teacher. Enjoy it, and take advantage of every opportunity. In case you are wondering, "Why am I talking to this child? He or she can't talk." The child may not have expressive language (verbalizing aloud), but the child has receptive language (understanding and receiving information). Children understand much more than we think. Just the other day I was keeping my one-year-old grandson. I said to him, "I'm going to take you for a ride in the stroller." He got up, went to the closet, got his shoes, and went to the door. Trust me, they understand.

The five senses are the five means we have to receive information. Everything we learn, we see it, hear it, feel it, taste it, or smell it. When we consciously receive information from one of these sensory avenues, we develop thoughts. From the thoughts feelings happen. From the feelings attitudes occur. From attitudes behavior is affected, and from habits, character forms and destiny is determined. How we use theses avenues of learning is crucial.

One day I heard an interesting illustration making an analogy between our children and computers. It went something like this: "Our children are like computers they are looking for the WiFi. They want connection." As parents we are that connection, sending out information for them to download. We have the responsibility to send out good information that has no bugs that would contaminate or defile. Our children are receiving information through their senses. We as parents have to work toward making what is received healthy.

It is important for parents to realize the importance of filtering or monitoring the input that goes into the use of these senses. What our children *see, hear, taste, touch, and smell* will have an effect on their lives or should I say destinies. In other words, what our children hear us say or hear someone else say or hears on the TV or computer has an effect on their lives.

We are very aware of the *sense of taste* and how it influences our lives. It is important to let our children experience various tastes. Sugar is a taste everyone likes and the baby will prefer sweets. So, introduce carrots, peas, and green beans before something really sweet. Be sure to get unsweetened fruit or grind fresh fruit.

Even though we prefer certain tastes, God has given us a variety of tastes in food, and we can learn to enjoy the variety. I have had parents say, "My child just likes ..." Perhaps the child prefers that taste, but as parents we need to encourage our children to try various types of food because they are good for us. When children say, "I don't like___," I smile and say, "You don't have to like it; you eat it because it is good for you." You are training the child to think of not only taste but nutrition. To be healthy we need to eat certain food. Just encourage the child to taste the food. Pushing food down the throat is not an option! A variety of food choices provides opportunities for your child to learn to appreciate and enjoy trying different food.

When it comes to the *sense of sight,* research is telling us to beware of what our children look at and how long because it is affecting the brains of our children. Research for yourself the effect these computer games and television is having on our children's ability to learn, concentrate, follow directions, pay attention, and other behaviors. Many disruptive behaviors are being manifest in our children in the classroom because of what they see.

Let us remember to teach our children to be thankful for their senses. If a child has a disadvantage in one sense, God strengthens another in a supernatural way. Remember, when we teach using all modalities, maximum learning takes place.

CHAPTER 5

I Am What You Call Me

One day a lady and her toddler came over for dinner. After we ate, we cleaned up the kitchen and the child wandered in while we were putting things away. With everything the child touched, his mom would say, "No. No, bad boy! No, no, bad boy." She must have said those words twenty times within the thirty minutes we were in the kitchen. My mind went wild as I thought of what that was doing to the child. All the child was doing was exploring— using his senses to learn. But what did the mother teach? She taught that when he touched things, he was a bad boy. The opportunity to teach the child about what he was experiencing and about acceptable ways to explore was lost. The words *bad boy* are etched in his brain. And you know what he has a greater potential to become? *A bad boy!* And his behavior is going to reflect that label.

Talking is one of the most important things a parent can do. Communicating with your child is so important, and what we say is *etched on the brain* for a long time.

The things we say to our children become life commandments. This term was coined by Dr. John Savage and introduced to me in one of his communication training seminars. As positive and effective parents, we should be sure to instill positive commandments. Over and over, I have heard some that are not so positive:

- You never do anything right.
- You are stupid.

- You will never be anything.
- You were a mistake.
- You will never be successful.
- I should have aborted you.
- You make me sick.
- You are always wrong.

And let's not forget the subtler messages we send, like "the terrible twos," "you never listen," and "you're so lazy." That's enough, right? But there are many more.

These words can fly off of our tongues without a thought but *become etched in a mind* forever.

I am reminded of a child who was told, "You will never be successful." This child grew up to be a pastor. He was able to increase the growth in a church in a matter of months. Whenever he noticed his success, he would always do something to mess up, and he would have to be moved to another church. This phenomenon happened three or four times. Someone suggested counseling for this young man. After some in-depth work, the counselor discovered the life commandment that was ruling the mind of this young man: "You will never be successful." Whenever he became successful, he would do something to keep it from happening. He would sabotage his success because he believed what he had been told. Powerful, huh?

Let's look at a few positive life commandments that would be better for our children to take with them for a lifetime.

- You are a gift from God.
- You are special.
- You are a hard worker.
- You strive to make good decisions.
- You are a good listener.
- I love you (say this one a lot).
- You bring joy to my life.
- You really thought through that problem.

- You can do great things.
- I am glad you are my daughter/son.

I am sure you can think of more. Children need to be affirmed daily. Choose to encourage your child, not to discourage. What we tell them they are is what they become.

I will never forget a little boy I had in my class one year. He had been labeled as a "problem child." I believe every child is smart and the challenge is to just study them and figure out *how* they are smart. So, the first day this child came to school I said, "You're a genius." I reaffirmed that all the time, and he had a great school year just because I looked at him differently.

I said you should say, "I love you," because many times it is taken for granted and not said at all. My husband says he doesn't remember hearing those words when he was a child. When we got married, he had to learn to say I love you and how to love.

Our children want to know they are loved. Your child needs to hear you say those words many times each day, even when he or she has done something wrong. That's unconditional love. I guess I really did not know the impact of unconditional love until one day when one of my daughters who had made some wrong choices said, "I know you and Dad really love me." It meant a lot to know even though she had hurt us a lot, unconditional love was able to shine through.

You may have some negative life commandments you need to get rid of. The first step is to admit it is having an effect on your life. You have to be willing to go against the adult who gave you the command. In other words, you must break the commandment. When you decide it is okay to break, you can put another in its place. Sometimes it is difficult to break a commandment, but it can be done. This negative command can have an influence on your parenting.

Let's concentrate on your role as a parent. Think of the many positive life commandments you can give your child. Enjoy building up your child.

Often when I present seminars, I have the parents get in a circle in a group of six.

I give each group a paper doll and say to them, "Pretend this is a child. I want you to say mean things to this child as you rip a piece off."

The members of the group pass the child around the circle, and each person says something mean to the child and tears a piece off.

After the doll is in shreds, I say, "Now I want each of you to say nice things and tape the doll back together."

When the groups hold up the doll, it's barely recognizable.

Then I ask, "What can we learn from this activity? Will that child ever be the same? Can you repair the damage? We cannot erase the damage that has been done. This is a powerful illustration of the power of words."

The Miranda Rule says, "Once a word is uttered, it cannot be retrieved."

Fortunately, the word *sorry* is a sorry word and cannot repair the damage done once a word is spoken.

Yes, you cannot take the words back, but you can strive to think before you speak and use words that heal and not hurt. Perhaps you are thinking about some words you have said to your child and you know these hurtful words have caused damage already. Here's what you can do. When you are alone with your child, apologize for your words in the past and express your love for him or her. It's best not to make promises, but from this day forward, ask God to guard each word that comes from your mouth and practice being positive. For example, if you have been calling your child lazy, saying he's always being slow when it's time to do homework, change your words to, "I know you are going to get that homework done quickly tonight." Watch what happens! When children know what we expect, they strive to do it. Then we must remember to affirm them with words like, "I knew you could do it."

God will forgive you for the past. Let's just keep the present and future loving, caring, and peaceful. Forgive yourself and remember you have the power to make a difference in your child's life.

CHAPTER 6

The Way They Should Go: Part 1 — Unique Gifts

I believe being a parent is the most important job on earth. I know I said it before, but it's worth saying again. As parents, we are faced with a decision: make our children in our own image or release our children to follow their God-given identities and live in the image in which He created them to be. We can accelerate or stifle, release or repress our children's giftedness. We should view each child as a book, not to be written, but to be read; not a blank slate awaiting a pen but codes to decode. Babies come with a preprogrammed hard drive according to their way. Proverbs 22:6 (KJV) says, "Train up a child in the way he should go and when he is old he will not depart from it." Remember the word *way* in the original Hebrew language refers to a unique capacity or characteristics, natural proclivity, and inborn distinctiveness. God has already "bent" your child in a certain direction. Study your child. Childhood tendencies forecast adult abilities.

As I think back on my girls, I see so many examples of this. My oldest daughter liked to color. If she could have a coloring book in her hand, she was happy. She could transform a coloring page by adding different shades, colors, and designs. She became an art director for an advertising firm, a graphic designer—using her skills designing.

My second daughter loved to paint. One time we had no paint around, and she made her own paint with Elmer's glue and food coloring and a painted a beautiful picture. It was so beautiful I kept it. That was over thirty-five years ago. She went on to receive a master's in fine art and works as an art teacher.

My third daughter liked to write when she was a little girl, and even before she could spell, she would fill up pages and pages of paper with scribbles. And as you might have guessed, I thought this was so cute I kept a few of her ring binders she filled with scribbles. When she was little, she would draw a picture and tell me, "This is me, Mommy. I am a writer." She would walk around with a pretend mic, as if she were interviewing people. She loved to talk and ask questions. Now she is a broadcast journalist and senior reporter for a radio station.

Study your child closely! His or her adult abilities are being revealed. The greatest gift you can give your child is not riches but revealing to him or her his or her own giftedness. God has a special work for each of us to bring him glory. Before you were born, God set you apart for a special work.

We are here for a purpose. Max Lucado says it this way: "God packed you on purpose for a purpose." Your child has been prepackaged. God has selected the temperament, the character texture, the yarn of his personality, all before he or she was born. God didn't drop your baby into your arms utterly defenseless and empty handed. Your baby arrived fully equipped. Your child is a gift, and your child is gifted. But we have to be careful here because the risk is to start thinking of your child as better than others, or less than someone else. Galatians 6:4 (NIV) says it this way: "Each person should judge his own actions and not compare himself with others."

When we make statements like, "Why don't you act like your sister?" Or "I wish you could just be more like your brother!" The child feels hopeless because he or she can't be like someone else. We have no choice but to be ourselves. Just remember to *never compare your children*—to another sibling or a friend's child or a stranger's child. God wants your child to be himself/herself.

Enjoy the journey as the child's giftedness is being revealed!

CHAPTER 7

The Way They Should Go: Part 2 — Understanding Temperaments

This part of "the way they should go" explores the topic of temperaments or personalities. I will be using those words interchangeably. Our children have been given special, unique gifts as well as special, unique personalities. Do you ever wonder why your child acts the way he or she does? Have you heard people say, "I have always been that way"? It is true we are born with a certain temperament and it influences every aspect of our life. I want to share some of my experiences.

Over thirty years ago, I attended a temperament seminar presented by Florence Littauer. This seminar changed my life. I don't know if I would be still married today if I had not attended that seminar. You see, my husband and I are opposites in temperament. I did not understand why he acted the way he did, and he did not understand me. When I attended this seminar, I began to understand him, and I learned to accept him as he is. We both learned that our differences can complement each other, and our differences provide variety in our lives. We are now celebrating forty-eight years of marriage, still learning to get along better. Now let me share with you some of the amazing things I learned about temperaments that helped me understand my husband and my children too.

I love being a mother. After I had my first child, Bill, the experience was so easy and wonderful; I thought I must be the best mother in the world. I said, "This parenting thing is a piece of cake! I could do this ten more times." If I didn't have any more children, I would have said I was a perfect parent and had a perfect child. I would be telling parents, "All you have to do is tell your children what to do and they'll do it." Then God blessed me with my second child, Nicole.

You see, Bill was compliant, calm, very peaceful, easygoing, understanding, happy, lovable, agreeable, and obedient, and he never said no.

Nicole came out screaming. She was outgoing, energetic, strong willed, and demanding, and when she spoke, her favorite word was no!

My third child, Lakisha, was quiet, serious, and intense. She slept through the night the first night home.

My third daughter, Priska, was lots of fun. She was bright and wide-eyed, curious, lovely, and cheerful.

I had always wondered how my children could be so different coming from the same parents. After I attended Florence Littauer's seminar, my eyes were opened—a truly exciting experience. In this seminar I discovered who I am and who my children and husband are. I learned the four temperaments, the personality types. When I understood my children's personalities, I found freedom to allow them to be themselves. I not only understood my children but my husband and myself.

In that seminar I learned there are four types of temperaments: sanguine, choleric, melancholy, and phlegmatic. The sanguine and choleric are extroverts, and phlegmatic and melancholy are introverts. I had four different children, and each one had a different type of personality. Each personality has its own strengths and weaknesses.

Florence Littauer says:

> Having a family is like putting on a production and the children are the cast. The only thing, we don't have a casting director who will put the right people into the perfect roles, so, the next best thing is to understand the cast we already have. Since I cannot predetermine the personality of each child I had we watch, observe and discover the personalities of each one of my children.

Littauer explains that each personality has goals, roles, directions, and needs.

Let's take a look at each personality.

Choleric

- Goals: Have control
- Roles: The director
- Directions: My way
- Needs: Achievement and appreciation

Sanguine

- Goals: Have fun
- Roles: The star
- Directions: The happy way
- Needs: Attention and approval

Phlegmatic

- Goals: Have peace
- Roles: The audience
- Directions: The easy way
- Needs: Respect and self-worth

Melancholy

- Goals: Have perfection
- Roles: The producer
- Directions: The right way
- Needs: Order and sensitivity

My son, Bill, is an *introvert*, a *phlegmatic*. In the cast his *role* is the *audience*. The personality *goal* for my son was to *have peace*. So if there is an argument going on, the tendency of my son would be to sit back and watch and encourage the group to settle it in a peaceful way. The *direction* of the phlegmatic is the *easy way*. He *needs* to be *respected* and *have self-worth*.

My first daughter, Nicole, is the *choleric*, an *extrovert*. In the cast her *role* is the *director*, her *goal* is to *have control*, and the *direction* for the choleric is *my way*. Her *needs* are *to achieve* and *be appreciated*. Nicole portrays herself as a leader and thinks her way is the best way.

The second daughter, Lakisha, is an *introvert—melancholy*. In the cast her *role* is the *producer*. Her *goal* is to *have perfection*, her *direction* is the *"right way"* and she *needs* to have *order* and *sensitivity*. This child is in the background as producer getting things done the right way.

The third daughter Priska is the *extrovert-sanguine*. In the cast her *role* is the *star*. Her *goal* is to *have fun*, and her *direction* is *"the happy way."* Her personality *needs attention* and *approval*. When she was joking around, naturally she wanted attention. Priska brought laughter to our home and made life fun.

As I began to internalize the *goals, roles, direction,* and *needs* of each one of my children, I could see the behaviors that depict those characteristics. Now I understood why my children were so different. They were born that way.

As I understood the different personalities, I realized this didn't happen by chance. Because I have a husband and children who were so different, I am able to accept all four types of personalities. All personalities are good.

Some may be easier to live with, but all of us need each other. We usually have a combination of personalities, but one is dominant. God knows how to combine the personalities to help us have a smoother and happier life. My husband is a choleric/sanguine. His desire to have control is balanced out with humor sometimes. In this chapter I am concentrating on one temperament at a time, not the combinations. I encourage you to study more to understand the combinations.

I had to be an organized mother. This organization included designing a learning environment for each one of my children.

The phlegmatic, my son, just wanted the peaceful way, so I knew he needed to be understood and respected to be happy. The choleric, my first daughter, wanted control, her way. I had to organize my life in such a way that I allowed opportunities for her to be in control and make decisions. The melancholy wanted the right way and everything to be perfect. As a parent I provided opportunities for her to organize things and make them "perfect." The sanguine wanted to have fun and what fun we have had. Did I do these things all of the time? Of course not. I'm not perfect! Those are examples to use to help the cast get along better.

I wanted perfection, peace and harmony in my home (I'm a melancholy/phlegmatic). I knew I had to work on it. *I understand now that being different is neither right nor wrong, it's just different. We all had to learn to understand our differences and accept each person as he or she is and not try to change each other.*

Sometimes as parents we try to change our children to be what we want them to be rather than letting them be themselves. I learned I should never compare my children. I taught each one to accept their sister or brother as they are. It is amazing to see the girls work on a project together and to see all their temperaments working. The director, Nicole, makes sure everything is in control; Lakisha, the producer, makes sure the event is arranged perfectly; and Priska plans the games and keeps everybody laughing.

I have benefitted tremendously from understanding temperaments. I now offer temperament seminars in schools, churches, and businesses. I want others to experience the joy of knowing why we act the way we do.

Understanding the personalities of my children and my husband has made my life free. When they react in a certain way, I don't have to wonder. I know they are being themselves. I remember people are different and being different is what? Neither right nor wrong! Right! You remembered. When we all learn to accept our differences, we can see we complement each other, and by working together we can make this world a better place.

If you have more than one child, they are probably very different. Enjoy discovering your child's personality. Now think about your children. Can you see some of the behaviors that depict these characteristics? In Florence Littauer's book *Raising Christians Not Just Children,* she has done an awesome job using a chart to explain each personality.

She has graciously allowed me to use these pages in her book. These pages were a great help for me to identify my child's personality. It is amazing to be able to identify the personality in your baby.

MELANCHOLY
-the Perfect Personality
(Deep blue like the ocean)

The Introvert	The Thinker	The Pessimist
Strengths		**Weaknesses**

BABY

Strengths	Weaknesses
Serious	Looks sad
Quiet	Cries easily
Likes a schedule	Clings

CHILD

Strengths	Weaknesses
Thinks deeply	Moody
Talented	Whines
Musical	Self-conscious
Fantasizes	Too sensitive
True friend	Hears negatives
Perfectionist	Avoids criticism
Intense	Sees problems
Dutiful and responsible	Won't communicate

TEEN

Strengths	Weaknesses
Good student	Depressed and withdrawn
Creative-likes research	Inferiority complex
Organized and purposeful	Inflexible
High standards	Suspicious of people
Conscientious and on time	Critical
Neat and orderly	Negative attitude
Sensitive to others	Poor self-image
Sweet spirit	Revengeful
Thrifty	Lives through friends
	Needs approval

Emotional needs: sensillvity to deep desires, sallsfaction from quality achievement, space to call his own, security and stability, separation from noisy, messy siblings, support from parents: ·1 believe in you:

Avoids: noise, confusion, trivial pursuits, being "Jollied"

PHLEGMATIC
-the Peaceful Personality
(Cool green like the grass)

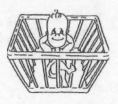

The Introvert   The Follower   The Pessimist

Strengths   Weaknesses

BABY

Strengths	Weaknesses
Easy-going	Slow
Undemanding	Shy
Happy	Indifferent
Adjustable	

CHILD

Strengths	Weaknesses
Watches others	Selfish
Easily amused	Teasing
Little trouble	Avoids work
Dependable	Fearful
Lovable	Quietly stubborn
Agreeable	Lazy
	Retreats to TV

TEEN

Strengths	Weaknesses
Pleasing personality	Quietly stubborn
Witty	Indecisive
Good listener	Unenthusiastic
Mediates problems	Too compromising
Hides emotions	Unmotivated
Leads when pushed	Sarcastic
Casual attitude	Uninvolved
	Procrastinates

Emotional needs: peace and relaxation, attention, praise, self-worth, loving motivation
Avoids: conflict, confrontation, Initiative, decisions, extra work, responsibility, tension, quarrels

SANGUINE
-the Popular Personality
(Bright yellow like the sun)

The Extrovert	The Talker	The Optimist
Strengths		**Weaknesses**

BABY

Strengths	Weaknesses
Bright and wide-eyed	Screams for attention
Curious	Knows he Is cute
Gurgles and coos	
Wants company	
Shows off	
Responsive	

CHILD

Strengths	Weaknesses
Daring and eager	No follow through,
Innocent	Disorganized
Inventive and Imaginative	Easily distracted
Cheerful	Short interest span
Enthusiastic	Emotional ups and downs
Fun-loving	Wants credit
Chatters constantly	Tells fibs
Bounces back	Forgetful
Energized by people	

TEEN

Strengths	Weaknesses
Cheerleader	Deceptive
Charms others	Creative Excuses
Gets daring	Easily led astray
Joins clubs	Craves attention
Popular	Needs peer approval
Ufe of the party	Con-artist
Creative	Won't study
Wants to please	Immature
Apologetic	Gossips

Emotional needs: attention, approval, affection, acceptance, presence of people and activity

Avoids: dull tasks, routines, criticism, details, lofty goals

38

CHOLERIC
-the Powerful Personality
(Hot red like a fire)

The Extrovert	**The Leader**	The Optimist
Strengths		**Weaknesses**

BABY

Adventuresome	Strong-willed
Energetic	Demanding
Outgoing	Loud
Precocious	Throws things
Born leader	Not sleepy

CHILD

Daring and eager	Manipulative
Productive worker	Temper-tantrums
Sees the goal	Constantly going
Moves quickly	Insistent
Sel f	Testing
-sufficient	Arguing
Competitive	Stubborn
Assertive	
Trustworthy	

TEEN

Aggressive	Too bossy
Competent	Controls parents
Organizes well	Knows everytlilng
Assumes leadership	Looks down on dummies
Problem solver	Unpopular
Self-confident	May become a loner
Stimulates others	Insulting
Excels In emergencies	Judgmental
Great potential	Unrepentant
Responsible	

Emotional needs: appreciation lor all achievements, opportunity for leadership, partici-pation In family decisions, something to control: own room, garage, backyard, dog

Avoids: rest, boredom, playing games he can't win

Read the chart carefully, and be amazed as you discover your child's personality.

The more we understand ourselves and our own temperament, the better equipped we will be to teach others. When we understand who we are, we are free to be what God wants us to be and to let others be themselves. Knowing the temperaments of my four children has helped me tremendously. We are able to accept each one!

I hope this chapter has helped you discover you child's personality. If you did not know about temperaments, I hope this information has been beneficial to help you discover your personality.

Marita Littauer, Florence Littauer's, daughter has written a book on *Your Spiritual Personality*: using the strength of your personality to deepen your relationship with God. It is fascinating to discover that our personalities affect our spiritual lives too! I continue to study to learn more.

My study of temperaments has led me to a booklet called *Understanding Your Temperament*: *A Self-Analysis with a Christian Viewpoint* by Peter Blitchington and Robert Cruise. This booklet shows how the four-temperament approach is relevant to every part of your life. They have conducted hundreds of studies, and they have shown that temperament plays a role in moral and spiritual development, academic development, vocational choice, popularity, ability to concentrate, and memory.

There is much more to learn about temperaments. As I mentioned earlier, we usually have two have temperaments, one extrovert and one introvert. One is more dominant. The stronger one has more influence on our lives. You might be a choleric/melancholy or sanguine/phlegmatic and so on. I believe God did this to balance out some of the stronger personalities. Occasionally a person will have two extrovert personalities or two introvert personalities. We all have a small percentage of each. Each personality has strengths and weaknesses. It is vital to know who you are so you can be in control of your actions.

Once I understood the four types, I had to understand how my temperament influences my parenting approach and the way I interact with my husband.

In Florence Littauer's book formerly titled *Raising Christians—Not Just Children* now called *Setting the Stage for Your Child's Faith*, she goes into detail with illustrations about how the parent-child relationship is affected by the temperaments of each one. I encourage you to continue your study.

Think for a moment, if you have a choleric personality whose main goal is to have control and you have a child that wants to be in control, guess what's going to happen? Unless you learn to accept each other, you will be in battle all of the time.

A parent who is phlegmatic and wants to have peace may find it challenging when disciplining a choleric child who wants control. This parent may have a tendency to give in to what the child wants to keep peace, especially when tired. Being aware of our weaknesses keeps us alert to avoid weakness pitfalls.

A parent who is melancholy wants perfection. When dealing with a phlegmatic child, you may find it challenging when the peaceful child couldn't care less about perfection.

The sanguine child wants to have fun. A choleric parent may not think it's funny when the child plays around when Dad wants him to do something *now*.

I hope this gives you an idea of the dynamics between the different personalities. Florence Littauer's book will go into detail with real stories of different combinations.

She tells a story about her phlegmatic son. She had gone over to visit. They were sitting and talking when the grandson came crawling into the room where they were. The baby was going straight to the dog food bowl. She thought her son would say something to the child, but he didn't. The baby's little hand went right into the dog bowl, grabbed a morsel of dog food, and popped it into his mouth. Naturally Florence said, "Son!" The son replied, "A little dog food never hurt anyone." He did not want to deal with a screaming child if he took him away. He could peacefully remove him now that the incident was over. Phlegmatic parents have to work hard to discipline consistently.

Children can easily see our differences, and if Mom and Dad fail to work together with the rules, the child will go to the easier parent to try to get what he or she wants. That's why it is so important to work together and be consistent.

I remember when my children were about seven, two, and four. My husband was in seminary, and I worked getting my PHT (putting hubby through). My husband's classes ended before I got home, so he picked up the children and went home. When they got home, my choleric husband was surprised when they dropped everything and started out to play. He said, "Wait a minute. You do your homework first, and then you can go play."

The children chimed in, saying, "But Mommy said we could play first."

My phlegmatic side wanted a little peace when I got home, so I let them play first. But Dad wanted to be in control. He let them play, but that evening we talked and discussed what our expectations for the children were, what the homework rules would be, and the many other things we needed to be in agreement on so our children could feel the consistency between the two of us.

Parenting is a journey, and as we live together, we must learn to accept each other just like we are. We are all *younique*! Enjoy the experience as you continue to accept, love unconditionally, learn, and grow together.

Oscar Wilde said, "Be yourself. Everybody else is taken."

CHAPTER 8

Why Am I Here? Spiritual Gifts

Being a teacher for over thirty years and a mother for forty-six years, I've found this understanding of spiritual gifts has given me profound insights into the behaviors and characteristics of my children. When I understand the child's essence, it gives me insights on how to teach and approach his or her learning. In this chapter I will give information to help you discover your child's "gift of essence"—how he or she will "be" in life. This is a revolutionary approach to help us understand our children and help them understand themselves and how we all fit together to make our world a better place.

It helps us accept each other's gift. We can see we need each other. Working together, we can have a taste of heaven on earth.

I will provide characteristics of each gift, which will bring clarity as to how behavior is influenced by these characteristics. When we see our children through the lens of spiritual gifts, we can feel good about who they are as they are revealing themselves to us.

This gift reveals how you will be in life: whether you are a doctor, teacher, singer, janitor, or whatever you will be in all works of life.

Remember Proverbs 22:6 (NIV): train up a child in the *way!*

God has already bent your child in a certain direction. Earlier I mentioned the *way* in the Hebrew; the original language refers to your child's natural bent. Read your child's God-designed itinerary. Discover your child's spiritual gift.

I repeat: the greatest gift you can give your child is not your riches, but revealing to your child his or her own giftedness.

God has given gifts each according to each one's unique ability. God endows us with gifts so we can make Him known.

"We have different gifts, according to the grace given to each of us" (Romans 12:6 NIV).

Let's look at Romans 12:6–8 and discover our gifts of essence. If a person's gift is *prophesying*, let the person use it in proportion to his or her faith. If it is *serving*, let the person serve; if it is *teaching*, let the person teach; if it is *encouraging*, let the person encourage; if it is contributing to the needs of others, let the person *give* generously; if it is *leadership*, let the person govern diligently; if it is showing *mercy*, let the person do it cheerfully. I am sure you have read those verses before. In this chapter, we will discover what they really mean and how they are manifested in our lives.

Remember, the gift of essence is different from the gift of function. This gift of essence shows how you will *be* in life. We know our children are gifts from God, so in this book we are looking at how God has gifted them to fulfill their purposes in life. This shows you what your *purpose* or mission is in life. Your *essence*!

Consider this illustration: I have a box of brushes—a hair brush, a paint brush, a toothbrush, and a wire brush.

- Look at the toothbrush. What is the purpose of the toothbrush? To clean teeth you say, right? Can it function in other ways? Yes! It can clean grout or clean shoes. But the creator of this toothbrush made it for the purpose of cleaning teeth (essence).
- Let's look at the hairbrush. What is its purpose? To brush hair. What would you think if I had a bucket of paint and was painting

with the hairbrush? That's not using it according to its purpose (essence). Or even worse, what if you saw me brushing my teeth with a wire brush? You'd probably think I was crazy! Right!

- Each brush was created by its creator for a certain purpose. That's its *essence*! The brushes can all function in different ways just as we can function in different ways, but our essence defines our purpose.

To illustrate, if the toothbrush wants to be a paintbrush, it would fail in the attempt because that is not its purpose. When we attempt to be something we are not—we may fail and find no contentment in who we are. When we discover our essence, we know why we are here and find fulfillment in being who we are meant to be.

It answers the questions, Why am I here? Who am I?

Remember the way your child will be as a singer, artist, doctor, pastor, engineer, and so on is revealed by his or her gift of essence.

As parents we must help our children unwrap their gifts—or maybe some of us parents haven't unwrapped our gifts yet.

We all have gifts.

The seven gifts listed in Romans 12 are *prophecy, service, teaching, giving, mercy, exhortation,* and *leadership.*

Each gift has certain characteristics that depict the way it will be in a given situation. There are misuses of each gift, and sometimes as adults we have to look at the misuses to determine the gift.

Perhaps you don't know what your gift of essence is and feel a little confused about now. Just stay with me, and as you discover your gift, you can help your child.

This model was adapted from Bill Gothard's model on spiritual gifts. He is the founder of the Basic Youth Conflicts Foundation. The characteristics and misuses of each gift come from Bill Gothard.

Have you ever wondered why it's so important for your child to tell who did what and when? The child who does this is usually called a tattletale.

This child has an innate code that tells him or her that he or she must proclaim truth and expose sin.

This child has the gift of prophecy. Take a look at some of the other characteristics and notice the misuses. Then it will become clearer for you what this gift is all about.

The Gift of Prophecy: Characteristics

- proclaims truth and exposes sin
- must express him- or herself
- loyal to truth
- forms quick impressions of people
- deep desire for justice
- alert to dishonesty

Prophecy: Misuses

- unforgiving
- condemns self
- dwells on the negative
- reacts harshly to sinners
- exposes without restoring
- gives up on those who fail
- jumps to conclusions

Do you have a child who loves to help? He or she is always there to help in whatever way he or she can. This child has the gift of service.

The Gift of Service: Characteristics

- meets needs of others
- meets needs quickly
- has difficulty saying no

- participates in short-range projects
- puts extra touches to jobs
- needs approval and appreciation

Service: Misuses

- gives unrequested help
- things are important
- tends to be pushy
- frustrated with rigid time
- works beyond healthy limits
- plans around own schedule

Have you seen the child who wants more information to prove what you are saying or just likes to argue over semantics? This child might say, "But teacher said …" Or "I read …!" He or she loves studying and getting more information.

The Gift of Teaching: Characteristics

- clarifies truth and validates information
- verifies information
- uneasy with subjective truth
- provides lots of data
- thorough/provides much detail
- uses original/primary sources
- clarifies misunderstanding

Teaching: Misuses

- proud of own knowledge
- interprets around self
- argues over semantics (minor points)
- relies heavily on credentials and shows off research skills

Then there's the child who turns problems into benefits and promotes spiritual maturity. That child seeks to please and assures you everything will be all right.

The Gift of Exhortation: Characteristics

- stimulates faith and promotes spiritual maturity
- sees the root of the problem
- turns problems into benefits
- solution oriented
- logical steps of action
- prefers face-to-face sharing

Exhortation: Misuses

- unrealistic goals
- boasts about results
- looks to self for solutions
- inappropriate sharing
- keeps others waiting on him or her
- prematurely starts projects

What about the child who feels for those who are hurting? This child is attracted to people in trouble. He or she takes up for friends who have done wrong. Sounds like the gift of mercy.

The Gift of Mercy: Characteristics

- stays with those who suffer—removes distress and shares burdens
- deeply loyal to friends
- possesses empathy for the hurting
- attracted to people in distress
- has a need for deep friendship

Mercy: Misuses

- becomes possessive: monopolizes time and attention of others
- leans on emotions only
- takes up offenses for someone who is being hurt by another person

- fails to be firm
- tolerates evil (may give sympathy and encouragement to those who are suffering as a direct result of breaking God's moral laws)

Have you ever wondered why you or your child is always thinking about the future or planning something that will happen later?

The Gift of Leadership: Characteristics

- plans ahead and completes tasks
- has plenty of energy
- visualizes final results
- cleans up after work
- decisive/able to delegate
- alert to details

Leadership: Misuses

- completes task quickly
- delegates to avoid work
- refuses to be accountable
- no interest once finished
- builds loyalty with favoritism
- unresponsive to others

Think of the child who is always giving in secrecy or investing in someone else's life. This child wants to give freely. This child wants to give without receiving. This child has the gift of giving.

The Gift of Giving: Characteristics

- entrusts assets and maximizes results—invests
- gives to answer prayer
- prone to give secretly
- personal thrift
- encourages others to give

Giving: Misuses

- hoards resources
- imposes high standards
- waits too long to give
- gives gifts to manipulate
- gives to projects, not people

I know this is a lot of information to digest. This is a topic I had to study in order to discover my spiritual gift. After this discovery I am free to be who I am. I have the gift of service. I knew I was happiest when I was doing for others. Now I know why. The gifts of essence determine how you will be in whatever profession you pursue. I often use the profession of a doctor to illustrate how each spiritual gift would determine how the person would be in that profession.

- A doctor who has the gift of prophecy would tell you *what you have done wrong and why you are in this condition.*
- The doctor who has the gift of service would be concerned about your *immediate need and what he or she can do to serve you.*
- The doctor with the gift of teaching would be *giving you pamphlets to read* about your condition or giving you websites *to get more information.*
- The doctor with the gift of exhortation would *encourage and give you hope for your future.*
- The doctor with the gift of giving *would be concerned about your financial needs,* if you have insurance, or need something. He or she would *give* you free samples of different drugs.
- The doctor with the gift of leadership would explain to you what *your future* would be like if you continue the lifestyle you have.
- The doctor with the gift of mercy would *be very concerned and assure you he or she will be there for you no matter what.*

This is another example of how the spiritual gift influences the response of each child. Let's look at a situation on the playground at school. The children were lined up waiting for a turn on the swing. The bell rang for the children to line up to go inside. One child snuck a swing quickly, unsupervised. The child fell and hurt himself. Seven children gave their responses. Notice how each gift manifests itself.

- The first child has the *gift of prophecy*. She comes running, saying, "I told you not to swing without the teacher! You would not have gotten hurt if you had come when the bell rang. Didn't you hear the bell? I'm going to tell the teacher."
- The second child has the *gift of service*. She runs to the child, saying, "Here, let me help you. I'll get a towel to wash you off and a Band-Aid. I'm going to help you."
- The third child has *the gift of teaching*. She comes with questions to gather data. "How did this happen? Have you done this before? Didn't you know this was dangerous?"
- The fourth child has the *gift of exhortation*. She comes to the child, saying, "You're going to be all right. Let's try it again. You can do it."
- The fifth child with the *gift of leadership* walks up with a concerned look on his face, saying, "If you want to finish school, you have to be careful. You could be crippled. You must be careful."
- The sixth child has the *gift of giving*. She says, "To make sure you won't fall and hurt yourself next time I'll *give* you my turn, okay?"
- The seventh child has the *gift of mercy*. He comes and sits down right by the hurt child and pats his back. He says, "They rang the bell too quick. They could have given you a chance to swing." The child stays close by, holding the child.

These are just illustrations to help clarify how each gift would respond in a given situation. Naturally all of us could respond in any of those ways, but the point is the given responses point out the characteristics of the specific spiritual gift. These responses would be the natural responses for each gift.

To assist you in discovering your child's gift of essence, the following questions will help identify some characteristics.

- What are some things your child likes about him- or herself?
- What troubles him or her most about life (in general)?

- What does the child do for others?
- What is the child good at doing/being?
- What does the child want to be or do?
- What areas of the child's life need to improve? This might bring out the weakness in a particular gift and can help you identify the gift. If the child is strong willed, the misuses may be seen more. These help you see what areas they need to work on.
- Are there particular areas of interest that you as a parent encourage him or her to pursue? Do siblings, teachers, and peers encourage the same? You are probably encouraging your child to pursue this particular thing because you see the gift.

Observation will help you identify the gift of essence in your child. Any opportunity as you observe your child will give you clues. As your child gets older, the following are a few suggestions for times when you may observe your child:

- in class during learning time and at home at play with sibling or friend
- on field trips, in the store, or at the park
- during group projects
- on the playground
- at a basketball game
- during center time, circle time, or playtime
- during class or family meetings
- during free time in the classroom

The study, discovery, and utilization of your spiritual gifts are basic and essential for fulfillment, joy, and satisfaction in life.

God has endowed each person with a specific mission or *purpose* to fulfill in life. The essence of God's will for each person's life is contained in his or her spiritual gift. Living based on our giftedness from God the Creator brings great joy and resolves the quest for meaning and our existence in the world.

Parents are to study and observe children and grandchildren, to gain insights into the child's *way* (nature, tendency, bent, proclivity). We add the observations and insights of teachers, grandparents, church members, peers, and other significant people in the lives of our children, to our own observations and gain an objective view. These observations help us discern the nature and character of the children and provide insight for discovery and identification of each child's gift. When our children were in school, teachers confirmed what we had seen in our children. The gifts of essence began to reveal themselves in elementary school. My son has the gift of teaching, my first daughter has the gift of mercy, my second daughter has the gift of exhortation, and my youngest daughter has the gift of service. What a joy it is as we see our adult children living out their gifts of essence.

Discovering your gift is an adventure, and because we are such complicated human beings, we really have to be honest with ourselves and each other, and we have to accept ourselves before telling others who they are. I have the gift of service, and my husband has the gift of teaching. We are so fulfilled when we are doing what we are made to be.

Once you accept who you are, you are free to be yourself and realize your *mission* for this life. Enjoy being you. You are the only you God made.

PART 2

The Joys of Parenting:
Experience Ways to Find Joy
in Everyday Experiences

CHAPTER 9

Labels, Functions, Purposes: Guide to Teaching

Remember every moment is a teaching moment! You have the opportunity to teach your child all the time. I am sharing guidelines to teaching. Whatever you are doing or whatever you are not doing, you are teaching. These are things to keep in the back of your mind all the time. When you are teaching, everything has a label, a function, and a purpose. Therefore, when you teach your child about things in the bathroom or kitchen, you will realize there are certain labels, functions, and purposes for things. You will be providing vocabulary for each of these categories.

For example, in the kitchen here are a few labels: the stove that has an oven, top burners, light to see inside, cabinets, sink, and refrigerator to name a few. Function includes: In the oven you bake or broil food. On top of the stove you boil, fry, or steam food. We wash things in the sink. We keep the food fresh in the refrigerator, and we store the food and dishes in the cabinets. You will explain to your child that Mommy has to cook in the kitchen so the family can have food. Notice all of the vocabulary you can introduce just by talking about things in the kitchen.

Remember talking to your child is so important. In every room of the house you can label everything. Count the steps on the stairways as you go up the stairway.

My oldest daughter says now wherever she goes she knows how many steps there are on the stairway because she unconsciously counts them. I guess that was a command I gave her and didn't know it.

Talk about the color of the walls and the name for each room as you pass by. You see, your baby is taking in everything you say, and you are developing a smart child with an enormous vocabulary. Your child's receptive vocabulary started in the womb, and by talking all of the time, you are developing more and more vocabulary. When your child's expressive vocabulary begins, you will be amazed and see the fruit of your labor.

In your child's room, you can literally label everything. On index cards, write the names of everything in that room and tape it to those items. To help you, this is a list of possible words: window, bed, chair, floor, ceiling, closet, wall, light, lamp, bookcase, toy box, pillow, sheets, etc.

When you do this, you are developing print awareness. Your child will see the words and associate the item with the word, and when he or she is old enough to read, he or she will already be able to sight-read the words.

One of the most important things you can do with your child is to read to him or her.

Read to your baby! Reading helps him or her develop vocabulary, syntax, grammar, print awareness, and the love of hearing your voice reading.

When your child learns to love words, reading, and books while he or she is young, it will continue throughout his or her lifetime.

Remember every moment is a teaching moment!

This saying is one I've found to be helpful: "Don't wait for the perfect moment; take the moment and make it perfect."

Join me as I share some things that brought me joy.

CHAPTER 10

Joys in Listening: Positive Communication

Talking to your child is very important, but listening to your child is just as important. In our society we have a tendency to talk at our children. "Do this, do that, hurry up, you need to eat, did you brush your teeth?" and so on.

How we communicate with our children determines the type of relationship we have with them. We must remember our children are just like us. We are just older. We all want to be understood, accepted, and loved. We as parents are the first to introduce love to our children. Did you ever think about that? You will show your child that love is constant or not, conditional or unconditional. Is love an on-and-off thing? Or is it something that happens when I am doing the right thing? Can I make a mistake and still get love? Am I loved only when I am good? Is love something I can turn on and off?

How we communicate with our children will determine their destiny. Now that is a powerful statement. Yeah, I am saying the words and actions we program into our children's lives will determine how they will be as employees, parents, and citizens in our world. That's why I said earlier parenting is the most important job in the world.

In the chapter on "I am What You Call Me" gets into the power of words in our children's lives. In this chapter, you were introduced to some specific ways to listen to our children that will promote healthy, happy, self-disciplined, self-controlled, responsible adults.

I think all parents want their children to know they will listen to them when they talk. We should never get too busy to listen to our children. Many children are crying out to be heard, and their behaviors reveal it.

In her book *How to Listen So Kids Will Talk,* Maryln Appelbaum at the Appelbaum Training Institute gives five things children need to open up.

1. "Children need to feel trust."

    If children can't trust us with their feelings, we will never know. So if your child says, "I hate you," it is natural to be hurt, but remember your child is saying this for his or her own reason. Be kind, be nonjudgmental, and encourage your child to say more. "Tell me more. What makes you feel that way?" is a good statement that proves to be helpful. Just listen!

2. "Children need to feel respected."

    "Everyone wants to feel important, honored, esteemed," says Appelbaum. "Praise the decisions your child makes. Support the opinions of children even if they differ from yours."

3. "Children need to feel safe."

    When children can say how they feel without being interrupted or condemned, then they feel safe.

4. "Children need to feel cared about."

    When people feel you care about them, they feel loved. A great way to show children they are loved is eye contact.

Let the love you have for them flow through their eyes. Ask God to let His love flow through you as you actively listen to your child.

5. "Children need to feel that they are important."

    As effective parents, we want our children's needs to be met. These five needs listed above give us insight into what needs are important to have positive communication and a good relationship with our children.

In communicating with your child, there are some words to avoid.

- don't
- why
- try
- but

Let's look at *don't* first. When I tell you, "Don't think of where you live," what did you think of? You probably thought of where you live. Did you do that on purpose? No. Our brains have trouble processing negatives. So when we tell our children, "Don't kick or don't run," they will probably kick or run. Are they being disobedient? No, they just heard kick or run. If you tell someone, "Don't be late," guess what? He or she will be late. So when we use *don't*, we are setting others up to fail. Instead we need *to say what you want them to do, not what you don't want them to do.* Instead of saying, "Don't run," say "Walk." Or instead of saying "Don't kick," say, "Keep your feet on the floor." Instead of, "Don't be late," say "Be on time." It is so powerful, and it works. Watch the use of *don't* as you speak today and see what happens.

The next word to avoid is *why*. Most people say, "Why?" What kind of word is why? It's questioning, condemning, maybe even interrogating. If I were to ask you, "Why did you wear that top you have on today?" You would probably want to explain to me why you did to explain your reason. Whereas when we use the words, *what's the reason, or tell me about, how did that happen*, we usually get more information, and the person doesn't feel like he or she has to prove him or herself and/or condemned. You've noticed I'm sure, when you ask your child, "Why did you do that?" the child shrugs his or her shoulders and says, "I don't know."

The next word is *try*. If I tell you to try to hold up your arm, you would either hold it up or leave it down. Try is a noncommittal word. If I ask you, "Can you come to the party tonight?" you could say, "I'll try," knowing you are not coming. I learned when I asked parents if they were coming to the parent meeting, 99 percent of the time they did not come if they said, "I'll try."

When we tell a child to try to be nice to his brother, he can say, "I *tried*!" But he wasn't kind to his brother. More positive words, such as, "I can, I will, I want to do …" get better results.

But is the last word on the words to avoid list. We know the word *but* is a disjunctive conjunction. In other words. it is the "eraser." We can say, "I really liked the picture you painted but …" What comes next will just erase what was said before, and the child will remember only the last thing that was said.

By the way, if you are commenting on your child's painting, it is best not to use an adjective to describe the picture. For example, instead of saying, "Your picture is beautiful, good, or nice," or try to guess what it is and get it wrong, comment on the picture. "You used a lot of color, or it is very colorful, lots of lines," or just say, "Wow, tell me about your picture!" This invites the child to share and express what is painted. Remember, you are showing interest and listening to the child when you use open-ended questions. "What is this? Tell me more. How does that work? Tell me who this is." These are questions that will invite communication.

When your child is a baby, it is really important to *talk to your baby*. Your talking to that baby provides an enormous receptive vocabulary so you will find that they are very verbal when they do start talking. When the child starts talking, however, then, it is time for us as parents to *listen!* We must encourage children to express themselves. When we do this, we are preparing for the future when they become teenagers, and you'll have open communication lines already in place. These open communication lines offer a freedom and assurance in your relationship with your child. If and/or when something happens at school, your child will feel free and safe to express his or her feelings. The problem can be resolved, and the dangers of bullying, damage of self-esteem, and school complacency will be alleviated or avoided.

Here are some thoughts to remember:

- The way we communicate determines what kind of relationship we will have with our children, spouses, and bosses—anyone, even the dog.
- Listening requires letting others know that we recognize the feelings behind what they are saying or not saying.
- Feelings are neither right nor wrong.
- By listening we can help others to think through an upsetting problem or situation.

To master positive communication, it takes practice, and many times it requires *change*. If we want our children to change, we must change first.

"When you change the way you look at things, the things you look at change," says Dr. Wayne Dyer.

When your child is talking and you are thinking about what you will do tomorrow, what you will cook for dinner, or what's coming on TV, you are not listening. Or you may be thinking of a counter statement to prove you are right; you are not listening. Listening requires observing the child's words, tone, and body language. You are considering the feeling your child might be having, and in your mind, you are coming up with tentative statements that reflect you were listening.

There are basically two types of responses: an open response or closed response. The open response requires you, the listener, to let your child know that you recognize the feelings behind what he or she is saying. By listening we can help the child through an upsetting problem or situation. We must remember that feelings are neither right nor wrong; they just are!

Here are examples of closed and open statements. A closed response denies children a right to their feelings by demonstrating listener's unwillingness to accept and understand.

Child: "I'm really disappointed with Billy and the other children for not coming over to play with me. There's nothing to do."

Closed response: "Well things don't always go the way you want them to. That's part of life."

Open response: "You're feeling left out—is that right?

The open response invited more communication, and the child can feel free to feel that way. Further conversation will allow the child to talk through what happened and what could change in his relationship with Billy.

Here are a few more open and closed responses.

Child: "I don't want to go to school today. Johnny is mean."

Closed response: "Everyone has to go to school. It's the law." (This gets preachy and overlooks feelings.)

Open response: "I sense you are feeling hesitant about going to school because of what happened last time with Johnny. Is that right?"

Child: "I wish I could go along. He always gets to go everywhere."

Closed Response: "We've discussed this before, so stop fussing about it."

Open Response: "You sound disappointed because you didn't get to go." (Allows child to figure out the problem as the conversation continues.)

Child: "I'm never going to play with her again."

Closed response: "Why don't you forget it? She probably didn't mean it."

(Tries to make excuses for other child and not allowing her child to express feelings about what happened.)

Open Response: "Tell me about what happened with her."

Child: "I can't do it!"

Closed Response: "Now don't talk like that. You just got started!" (Sounds encouraging but doesn't allow child to express feelings behind the "I can't.")

Open Response: "What happened that made you feel that way? Let's see what happens when you keep at it."

Child: "You're the meanest mother in the world!"

Closed Response: "Don't you ever talk to me that way!"

Open Response: "I really feel hurt when I hear those words. It sounds like we need to talk." (Here an "I" message was used, a skill I will discuss next.)

These examples allow children to express their feelings, but what about the parent's feelings? Yes, there is a way to express our feelings without accusations, inferences, judgments, or name calling. You can make a direct expression of your feelings using a skill that's called "I messages." Instead of using the attach word "you," the "I" message calms down a situation and allows the speaker to vent in a kind way. Here are some examples.

You Message: "You always throw your clothes on the floor!"

I Message: "I am upset when I see clothes on the floor after I've cleaned up."

You Message: "You are so rude. You are always interrupting when I'm talking."

I Message: "I find it very difficult to keep from screaming when I get interrupted while I'm talking." (You get to express how you are feeling without name calling.)

You Message: "You always make me late."

I Message: "I feel so embarrassed when we are late. I would be so happy when we get to church on time."

Sometimes when I talk about "you" messages and "I" messages, someone might say, "Who talks that way?" I say it takes practice and a willingness to change. I'm not perfect and sometimes find myself resorting to name calling. Just tonight I told my husband he was moping about something I said earlier. He was, but it wasn't kind to say that to him. If I had said something like this, "I sense you feel sad about something I said. Is that right?" we probably would have had a better evening. So stay encouraged, never give up, and keep improving and learning.

Let us be mindful of the *words* we speak! My husband and I have workshops for parents called, "Learning the Language of Healing." These workshops help the participants learn to use words that heal, not hurt. The theme scripture is Proverbs 12:18 (NCV) "Careless words stab like sword thrust but the wise words bring healing."

Let's think about how careless words sound.

- I hate you.
- You never do anything right.
- You are stupid.
- You are mean.
- You'll never be anything.
- You will always be fat and ugly.

Words that heal:

- I love you.
- You are special.
- Thank you.

- I appreciate you.
- You are so creative.
- You a gift from God.
- You can do it.

Careless words and wise words can be characterized in the following ways.

Careless words

- unthinking
- inattentive
- thoughtless
- inconsiderate
- unmindful
- unconcerned
- negligent
- slipshod
- hasty
- unwise

Wise words

- tending to cure/healing
- remediating
- prudent
- sensible
- judicious
- clever
- intentional

Each time I open my mouth, I must intentionally think of uttering words that heal not hurt.

There's another proverb that reminds me of my use of words. "A gentle answer will calm a person's anger, but an unkind answer will cause more anger" (Proverbs 12:1 NCV).

When I find myself getting angry, I've found there is one quick way to calm myself down. *"Breathe!"* When I concentrate on breathing, my desire to scream or raise my voice is controlled, and a mutually beneficial outcome (MBO) is achieved. In my husband's book *The Gift of Criticism*, he coined those words. Whenever we are talking to someone, it should be our desire to have a MBO. In his book he stresses the importance of change in our lives. As parents we will find out that when we change, our children change.

Our children are smart, and they know what to do to push our hot button. When we change our responses and do something different, it throws them off, and because you have changed, they change. Instead of screaming and hollering at our children, we can *breathe* and watch what happens.

Occasionally there is a gap in our communication. It can be called an interpersonal gap. It happens when we say something and the child or any person basically misunderstands what you said or looked at the words you spoke in a different context. When a gap occurs, it is our responsibility to resend or clarify the message to help the person understand.

I remember I was telling my preschool class in Genesis about creation. I said that God through Jesus made the world. A child raised her hand and asked, "Where did God throw Jesus?"

I remember when I was a child, I came into the kitchen and asked my mother for something to eat. She responded by saying, "You'll spoil your appetite." I accepted that answer but later came in the kitchen and asked, "Mommy what are we going to have for dinner, appetite?" These are gaps in understanding. One day we were eating watermelon and my grandson asked, "Why do they call it *water*melon?" It is our responsibility to clarify what has been said and not put the child down or laugh at his or her response.

Thoughts to Remember

- Children become what we call them.
- Children become what we expect them to be.
- We are to model what we want our children to become.
- Be consistent,
- Say what you mean; mean what you say.
- Avoid threats.
- Be cautious about bargaining or bribes.
- Program first-time responses from your child.
- Teach and model accountability.
- The person who is talking is telling you what to say. So *listen well!*

CHAPTER 11

Joys in Discipline

Probably the first thing that needs to be cleared up is the difference between discipline and punishment. Some people think to discipline a child is to punish her. Some think punishment is a form of discipline. I would say both are incorrect. Discipline comes from the root word to *disciple*, to make a follower. Some years ago, I started using this format to explain the difference between discipline and punishment. I don't remember where the layout came from, so I don't know the author to give it credit to. Consider this explanation:

Root word: disciple/learner

Discipline: training that develops self-control

Punishment: punitive action triggered by your anger

Discipline

Purpose: To train for correction

Focus: Correct future deeds

Attitude: Love and concern on the part of the parent

Outcome: Security and trust

Punishment

Purpose: To inflict pain or hurt

Focus: Past deeds

Attitude: Hostility and frustration on the part of the parent

Outcome: Fear and guilt

Basic Principle: When *love* is applied in all discipline, the child's self-esteem is always considered. It is always important to consider the impact of words on the child.

Communication (verbal or nonverbal), once transmitted, cannot be retrieved.

So we can say discipline is a joy or should be a joy. You have the opportunity to train your child to have self-control.

Kay Kuzma, in her book *A Hug, Kiss, and a Kick in the Pants*, presents a creative approach to preventing disciplinary problems.

She reminds us to keep our child's love cup full by doing the following:

- Give attention: Children equate love and attention.
- Be a good example in word and action.
- Use words that protect and preserve children's feelings that they are lovable and capable.

You have the power to change your child's misbehavior by simply filling his love cup!

Kuzma tells us how to empty your child's love cup.

- Be too busy to give attention.
- Use a child's name in a negative manner.

So, instead, fill your child's love cup!

- Use encouraging rather than discouraging words. ("You can do it," not "Is it too hard?")
- Use positive rather than negative suggestions or statements. ("Close the door gently," not "Don't slam the door!")
- Use specific rather than general statements. (For two- and three-year-olds, say, "Put your socks on. Now put on your shoes." Don't say, "Put on your clothes.")
- Use manual guidance to aid verbal suggestions with the young. (Take the child by the hand and say, "Please sit down here," not "Sit down!")
- Avoid issues with children. Discuss misconduct in private.
- Avoid making *threats*. If they are not followed through, undesirable behavior is reinforced. If you must carry out threats, everyone is hurt.

Threats and bribes are often used to try to get our children to do what we want them to do. I'm guilty of saying, "Eat you dinner and you'll get a cookie." I should want my child to eat their dinner to be healthy, not just to get a cookie. Should a cookie be their motivation to eat? My married daughter has two children. She decided desserts were getting out of hand at dinnertime and she wanted to cut down on sweets. So she decided to have dessert twice a week after dinner. Having dinner without a dessert sounds like a healthy idea, doesn't it? She announced the decision, gave her reasons, and followed through. Now when they visit, I have to check and see if dessert is okay.

I remember one day I saw a parent trying to get her two little girls in the car after shopping. The girls were running around the car laughing while Mother screamed, "Get in the car; don't be running around like that." The girls ignored her, and she bribed them by saying, "Okay, okay, I'll stop by McDonald's and get you something. Come on and get in the car." Of course the girls got in the car. She bribed her children to get them to do what she wanted done. A threat would have sounded like this: "If you don't get in the car I'm going to …!"

So a threat and bribe does the following:

- gives a condition
- promises something to stop the behavior
- makes a deal (If you do this, I'll do that ... If you don't do this, I'll do this.)
- masks embarrassment (in store, doctor's office, church, etc.)

So what's the answer to getting your child to do what you want him or her to do?

Teaching responsibility requires intentional teaching. Mom and Dad or two people who are responsible for your children should make a list of expectations. Decide on logical consequences that would teach your child to be responsible and carry out your expectations. After each person agrees, the expectations and consequences should be discussed with the children.

A part of discipline is helping our children see that there are consequences in life. There are natural consequences like if you touch a hot stove, you get burned or jump from a high place you might fall and get hurt. Then there are logical consequences that are directly related to the behavior. When a child is told to do something and he or she chooses not to follow the instruction, there is a logical consequence that follows. In Kay Kuzma's book, *A Hug, a Kiss, and a Kick in the Pants,* she shares a story about a morning episode with her children. She had a son who wanted to make her late every morning it seemed. When he was told to get up, he didn't get up until about the fourth time. Then he would go really slowly until it was time to go and his mother had to wait on him. Well, one morning this mother decided to tell her child one time to get dressed. The time came for them to leave for school and the child was not ready. The child grabbed his clothes and had to dress in the car. Somehow one sock was missing. The child had to be in school with one sock. The consequences of the behavior were clear. The child learned to get dressed when Mom said so. When there are logical consequences, the child understands and behavior changes. When you use the logical consequences approach, it is important that you have talked to your child beforehand and he or she knows what will happen. I recommend having a family meeting. In this meeting, parents should do the following:

- clarify expectations
- decide on the logical consequence that will go with each behavior/ situation
- have the child verbalize the agreement (all ages)
- decide on weekly checkups

Here are some examples of logical consequences:

- Child does not come when called to dinner. He or she misses dinner that evening.
- Child doesn't clean up toys. Toys are put away for a while and an agreement is made that if he or she wants to play with toys, they will have to be put up. Or for the older child, perhaps a fine is paid to get the toys back, and if it is not paid, toys are given away. Be sure this arrangement is made before the behavior happens and that the child knows what to expect. Therefore, a mutual agreement is made, and the child can see that you are training him or her to be responsible. Otherwise the child will feel like you are being mean, punishing, getting back, or even that he or she is unloved.
- Child does not want to eat what you have for dinner. He or she chooses to go hungry.
- Child takes too long to get ready for bed. He or she loses the chance for a story.

This is developing a responsible child. Your child knows he or she can trust you to do what you say and the consistency develops love between you and your child.

I must repeat, it is vitally important to have family meetings and talk over all of the consequences for a certain behavior. This shows love and consistency on the parent's part and provides a loving atmosphere in the home. One of the most powerful books I have read that addresses logical consequences is a book by Foster Kline and Jim Fay called *Parenting with*

Love and Logic. They have incredible illustrations to help parents know how to use logical consequences. They introduce a foolproof system that works. The authors believe their methods give children the opportunity for a joyful, productive, and responsible adult life.

We must show unconditional love in all situations: at home, at work, at church, in the grocery store, at the park, wherever we are. I often ask parents, "Are you as kind to your child as you would be to a guest in your house?" Then I say, "If your guest spilled their drink at the dinner table, how would you respond?"

You would probably say, "Oh that's okay, we will clean it up." If your child spilled their drink at the dinner table, how would you respond? Tell the truth! Would you resort to name calling, yelling, put downs? Would it sound like this: "You are so clumsy. You are always knocking things over, and you never do anything right!" Or could you say, "Wow, let's clean that up. We'll have to practice being more careful. Here, I'll help." This acknowledges that the child may have done this before and you are aware of that but does not make the child feel like he is so incompetent and usually does nothing right. Words that are put downs makes the child to believe he'll never please you and feel hopeless. The children will also notice how you respond to the guest and feel they are not as important as the guest. Whenever we open our mouth, we must guard our words and consciously choose words that heal not hurt.

Remember discipline with love is the answer!

CHAPTER 12

Joys in Worship

I teach that everything we do is worship to God or to the enemy. However, a special place and time to come together as a family brings joy. It's a time to let God know we love Him so much that we want to pause as a family once or twice a day to say thank you, sing, and pray to him and learn scriptures together. This was really a special family time for our family. I play the clarinet and autoharp, my husband plays the piano, and two of my daughters play the violin. You can imagine the times we had together singing and playing our instruments. The daughter who didn't play an instrument enjoyed singing. Today she writes songs for our choir to sing. I thank God for music and the freedom we have to worship him in this country.

The length of family time doesn't matter. It depends on the day, how late it is, your schedule, and other realities. Once we tried having worship time at the same time every day, but as the children got older with different schedules, we would just have worship when everybody was home. One time one of our children really let us know how important worship was to her. We had gone out somewhere, and she had fallen asleep in the car. We were going to slip her clothes off gently, trying not to wake her, and all of a sudden, she abruptly sat up and said, "We didn't have worship!" We smiled and gladly had worship time together.

Choose the worship format that works for your family. It's a time the whole family will look forward to coming together. We found that singing, studying scripture, reading a Bible lesson/acting out a story (as your children get older, they can lead in worship, tell a personal experience, or read a Bible story or scripture), and prayer was a format that worked for us. There were times when it was late and everybody was tired, so we'd have a song and prayer. The important thing is that you do it. It didn't matter the order.

The baby will look forward to your worship times too. I have recordings of my baby at five months singing at worship. It was just noise of course but a *joyful* noise. My last daughter liked to write poetry, and sometimes she would share a poem at worship. The daughter who writes songs would teach us her song. It's just a wonderful experience if we let the time be flexible, involving the whole family. When the baby is little, sweet, repetitive songs are good, but whatever songs you like to sing, the baby will learn them. You will smile one day when you hear your baby singing a hymn you sing often.

When the baby gets big enough to clap, the song, "Jesus loves the little ones like me, me, me," found in the song book called *Little Voices Praise Him* published by Review and Herald Publishing Association is a song my children really loved. When your children get older and have their own repertoire, you will be singing their favorites most of the time. It doesn't matter how your voice sounds. Your baby will think it is beautiful, so sing to your baby. Music is joy to the soul.

Plato says it like this: "Music gives a soul to the universe, wings to the mind, flight to the imagination and life to everything."

Sing when you are happy, sad, or mad. You will find singing will help. Sing songs to Jesus and about Jesus.

I wrote a song titled, "I'm Special," found in the back of the book. This song teaches children they are special and that *God* made them. It is important for our children to know who made them and they are loved and special.

When you have this special family worship time, your child will learn how to behave in church when you experience corporate worship.

If you have more than one child, there's no need to worry about the age difference. Coming together as a family is the important thing. The format is not as important as the act itself. Children are very flexible, and they like repetition. You might be tired of that song or story, but they won't be. I have four children, so they liked taking turns leading, choosing the songs and scriptures, or even acting out a Bible story.

We enjoyed memorizing long scriptures together. The New International Version or New Century Version are usually comfortable for the children. The Children's International Bible is helpful when they are young. To name a few: the twenty-third Psalm, Psalm 139, Proverbs 3:5–6, Romans 12:4–8, Philippians 4:13, John 14:1–3, and John 3:16–17. It sounds like a speech choir when you say it together. It is so wonderful just hearing everyone reciting the word of God.

Prayer time is a time when the family can share concerns, thanks, confessions, and petitions.

When our children see the power of prayer, their faith is strengthened. I remember when I was around seven, I would walk in my sleep. My mother said, "We have to pray about this." She stopped me one night as I was getting ready to go out of the door. I was also planning a trip to visit my cousin who lived on a lake. Naturally as mothers do, she could just see me sleep walking right into that lake. So we prayed, and I never walked in my sleep again. That really strengthened my faith, and I have experienced the power of prayer in miraculous ways. Because my prayer life was so strong, my children learned at an early age to believe in prayer.

I remember an occasion when we had a bunny that got out of the yard and ran away. When the children found out, they said, "Let's pray and ask God to send him back." As parents do, I explained that God might want someone else to have the bunny or something could have already happened to the bunny. Anyway, they prayed. Three days later, we were going out of the door to go to church and there the bunny was sitting on the steps. God did answer their prayer.

On another occasion, we got stuck in some mud. It was really bad. The car wheels were so deep in the mud you couldn't see them. The children said, "Jesus can get us out!" We prayed and waited for a few minutes. I thought Jesus would send somebody by to pull us out. Well, I decided to try to get the car out again. The mud splattered on the car and did not move. Then all of a sudden, there was a force that pushed us backward out of the mud. The children screamed, "Jesus got us out of the mud!" The faith of children is awesome!

I do teach my children that God always answers prayers. Sometimes His answer is yes, sometimes it is no, and sometimes it is wait a while. We want our children to know prayer is simply talking to God, and He is always listening. When you experience answered prayers, be sure to share them with your children. Just the other day I was driving my car, and I felt impressed to pray, "God, please help me get home safely." A moment after that prayer, my car stopped and wouldn't start. God knew I was just five minutes from the body shop where we get our car repairs. I called the gentleman up, and quickly he was there to my rescue. My gas gauge wasn't working properly, and I just needed gas. He got gas for me, no charge, and I was on my way singing praises to God. I immediately called my family and shared the news of how God had my back. We don't have to worry! We must always remember that God is always with us, and He wants the best for us. As we trust him we will find He "is able to do exceeding, abundantly above all that we can ask or think" (Ephesians 3:20 KJV).

Whenever I think of this scripture, this prayer story comes to mind. I'll attempt to condense it. When my husband was in seminary in Michigan, our car decided to fall apart. Worst of all, the heater went out. In those frigid temperatures in Michigan, you really *need* a heater. My husband prayed for time and money to fix up this old car that had over two hundred thousand miles on it. Well time went by, and we never had time or money. I would wrap the children in blankets and scrape windshields when we would drove forty miles away to work in a church.

One summer my husband was working, taking the census, and he went to a farmhouse and met a lady who invited us over to visit her after she found out my husband was a seminary student. We would visit her, sing songs, and have prayer with her. She was very kind to us, sharing apples, cherries, and tomatoes from her farm. Months passed and one day we got a call from that lady. She said she was compelled to buy a car for us. We were amazed! The car dealer was too! He said, "I filled up the tank, so ride a while." I guess he just wanted to add to our blessing. It was a brand-new Buick LaSabre. She paid the taxes, tags, and insurance for that car. God is to be praised!

Now you can understand why Ephesians 3:20 (KJV) brings to mind that story. When Bill prayed about fixing up the old car, his prayer had already been answered. Instead we got a brand-new car. That was *exceedingly, abundantly above all we asked or thought to ask*! God loves us more than we can imagine. Pray bold prayers! God can handle it!

Enjoy praising God. He is worthy to be praised!

To add variety to prayer time during family worship, find ideas in the appendix.

How or when you use the ideas will be determined by the size of your family and the age of the children.

CHAPTER 13

Joys in the Bathroom

Children are fascinated with water, and one of the safest places is in the bathroom with *you*. I emphasized *you* because *it is important that you accompany your child in the bathroom*. Accidents can happen in the bathroom, so I preface this chapter with this warning. Now I *said joys in the bathroom. Where is the joy? Here goes.* When you bathe your infant/child, do the following:

- Feel the warm water.
- See the water and bubbles.
- Hear the sounds the water makes when running into the bathtub, how the water sounds when you splash the water, when the toilet flushes, listen to the sound water makes when it runs down the sink. This develops sound awareness and auditory skills needed to read and become phonetically aware of the sounds letters make.
- Let the child feel the bar of soap and explain the purpose of soap. Let her know the soap is to clean with.
- Have something to blow in the water. A straw is fine, or if there are bubbles, just blow the bubbles and watch what happens.

When your child becomes a toddler, you can have different-size cups to pour in. Measuring cups varying in size bring awareness of how many cups of water are needed to fill one or a half cup.

Bathroom mirrors are great to look in. This is a good place to teach self-awareness. Teach the body parts, including the genitals simply as a part of the body with a name, just like the other parts of the body. Lots of times I have seen parents teaching body parts when they are changing the baby's diaper. They begin touching parts and saying their names and the baby touches the parts, and that's okay until the child touches the penis or vagina, and then they take their hand away or even spank that hand and say, "Don't touch that!" It doesn't even get a name, and the child feels like it's something bad to touch. When penis and vagina are taught along with leg, feet, arms, and the other parts of our bodies, these are just body parts with no negative connotations. What is the reason terms like "wewe" and "teetee" are taught when later on because of confusion of these terms, we have to explain them? I believe children have a healthy self-image when each part is taught in a positive way. When a boy child knows he holds his penis when he goes to urinate, he can learn to be thankful that he can go to the bathroom. Later he can learn other things about his penis, just like learning to write with his hand. The little girl can be thankful for her vagina now and learn when she urinates, water will come from it. We know it's coming from the bladder, but you know what I mean. Later she will learn other wonderful things about her vagina. When there is nothing to be ashamed of, a child can have a healthy respect for his or her body parts.

The book *Thank You God for My Body* teaches the body parts, and it draws the child's mind to God, who made that part of the body. I wrote this book when my last child was a baby. I had been looking and looking for a book to teach the body parts and about God who made our bodies. I ended up writing it myself.

Sometimes the bathrooms have fans that make noise. Turning them off and on bringing out the sound difference is a teaching time.

Lots of fun things can be taught in the bathroom!

> *Warning!* Never leave your child unattended in the bathroom until
> you know for sure he or she is old enough to be safe alone.

CHAPTER 14

Joys in the Kitchen

The kitchen is a place we may spend lots of time, especially if you like to cook like I do. When my children were babies, I would sit them in the infant seat on the cabinet. This is where their interest in cooking developed. Now all of my children are good cooks, including my son. While your child is sitting in that infant seat watching, you have the opportunity to teach math, science, health, social studies, music, and many other subjects I am sure you can think of.

Include lots of vocabulary. Remember, the receptive language develops first, and even though your child does not talk, he or she is learning.

Whatever you are doing—cooking, cleaning, washing dishes, or mopping—you are the teacher. Whatever you are doing, safety is important. As your child gets older, rules change. Explain that some things are to look at, some are to touch, and some are to taste. Your child will learn about temperature when you explain some things are hot and some are cold. He or she will learn to stay away from hot things. Hopefully he or she won't have to experience hot before he or she believes you.

The vocabulary is numerous in the kitchen. Just to name a few kitchen words: refrigerator, freezer, shelves, drawers for fruit, vegetables, handle on door, oven, stove, burners, cabinets, sink, water faucet, countertop. When you go near these things, tell your child what they are, their function and purpose. For example: we bake in the oven, and we boil, fry, and sauté things on the stovetop. If you'd like, write the words on index cards and tape them on the appropriate item.

Since baking bread is my favorite activity in the kitchen, I will share some of what I call, learnings in bread making. Bread making provides valuable experiences to enhance the learning and development of your child. Bread making should be semi-structured to guide your child in learning and ensure fun in the dough. Initially your baby will be observing you make bread. When it is in dough form, the baby can touch the dough as you talk about how soft it feels or how warm or cold it feels. Of course, you will be talking, talking, talking and exposing your child to much vocabulary. I am including a list of vocabulary words to keep your memory fresh. When your child begins to talk, he or she can repeat some of the vocabulary words. When your child has developed the vocabulary, you can ask questions and allow him or her to respond.

Your child can learn that a recipe tells the ingredients that are in whatever you are making. Go over the list of ingredients, and when the child is old enough, she can repeat after you. I made up a song using the tune "The Farmer in the Dell." If you don't know that song, make up a tune and have fun. Or Google it!

Here are the words for the song I made up: *"We're making bread today, making bread today, praise God in heaven, we're making bread today."*

I tell the child that God has made all of the things we will use in the bread so we can make bread, and give God praise.

The next verse goes like this: *"We put flour in the bread, flour in the bread, praise God in heaven, flour in the bread."*

Another song that brings out where the ingredients come from using the same tune,

goes like this: *"God made the wheat for flour, made the wheat for flour, praise*

God in heaven, God made the wheat for flour. God made the bees for honey, made the bees for honey, praise God in heaven, He made the bees for honey."

God made the sea for salt, etc. Put whatever the ingredients are in the song.

If you have an ingredient that doesn't fit the song, just talk about it and leave it out of the song. When it comes to kneading the bread, there is another song using the same tune, "The Farmer and the Dell." If you don't know the tune, Google it.

Here goes: *"We're kneading bread today, kneading bread today. This is the way we knead the bread, kneading bread today."*

The same tune can be used to sing these words: *"Turn, fold, and push, turn, fold, and push. This is the way we knead the bread, turn, fold, and push."*

Vocabulary and baking terms that can be taught are numerous. To name a few: *recipe, measuring spoon/cups, knead/kneading, stir/stirring, pour/pouring, bake/baking.*

Actions: grease pan, knock down, shape

Science: liquid, solid, temperature (cold, lukewarm, hot), salt from the sea, bees from the honeybee, flour from wheat

Textures:

- smooth, rough, thick, sticky, soft, gooey
- wet, dry

Think of what you can teach in math!

Some mathematical concepts are:

- How many: counting
- Height: How high did the dough rise?
- Volume: Will the dough fit in pan?

- Directions: turn, fold, push
- Measurements: 1 cup, 1/2 cup, 1/4 cup, teaspoon, tablespoon, etc.
- Sets: dry ingredients and wet ingredients

Think of what you could teach in science!

- How yeast works—it makes bread rise.
- What honey does—it makes bread taste sweet. (Explain chemical reactions to an older child.)
- Where flour comes from. (Use books to illustrate, such as *Thank You God for My Body*, or get fresh wheat.)
- How honey is made—by bees. (Use library books or use the internet and find pictures of a beehive or make a beehive. Let your Child taste the honey if over 12 months old. (American Academy of Pediatrics advises)
- How oil is made—where it comes from. (Explain that the oil we use comes from vegetables.)
- Where salt comes from—the sea.
- Teach the process of how a liquid becomes a solid.

Think of what you can teach in health.

Vocabulary: whole wheat flour/unbleached flour

When my children were around three or four, they were making bread every week. They learned the importance of using whole wheat flour. I used a diagram to show how the whole kernel provides many more nutrients. There are twenty-plus nutrients in the outer shell of the wheat. When we eat only the white flour, we miss all of the many important nutrients, such as bran, biotin, and many more. On the white flour bag, they call the white flour enriched because they have put back in the flour four nutrients that were lost when the outer part of the kernel was removed. I ask this question: If you let a person borrow twenty dollars from you and they gave you four dollars back, would you feel enriched? Are we being deceived or what?

As parents we must read labels and be very aware of the false advertising that is being presented to us. In the bread recipe, I use honey instead of sugar. Honey is sugar made by the bees, and our bodies use it differently than processed sugar. High fructose corn syrup (HFCS) is being put in many foods, including fruit juice for children. Diabetes is developing in so many because of this killer, HFCS. We must also remember bread and carbohydrates turn into sugar in our bodies. Therefore, it would be wise to avoid white flour, white rice, white bread, white spaghetti—you get the point.

When your child grows out of the infant seat, a special cabinet with baby-proof things in it would be helpful. Choose a cabinet away from the stove and have items like wooden spoons, plastic containers of different shapes and sizes, a few small glasses or bowls, etc. Some of the cooking you do your child can help with, but sometimes because it is unsafe or you just don't have time, that cabinet of things will come in handy. Tell the child it is there just for him or her and he or she can use his or her imagination and pretend he or she is cooking. It will seem special.

Just remember, getting your kitchen messy is part of it all. This is the opportunity to teach your child how to clean your kitchen.

My grandson likes cleaning up because of the opportunity to play in water. Give your child a wet sponge to clean the table or countertop. As they get older children can help put dishes in the dishwasher or rinse them in the sink.

The important thing is you are spending quality time with your child that will be remembered for the rest of your lives. Just relax and enjoy the time and have joy in the kitchen.

You can find recipes in the back of my book *Thank You God for My Food*. The recipe for sugarless apple pie and whole wheat biscuits is delicious. Try it!

Food for thought!

Since it has been such a long time since I started this book, the processing of food has changed tremendously, and I feel I must add a warning. Much of our food today has been genetically modified. I still make bread, but I make sure the flour is organic and non-GMO. Jeffrey M. Smith's book *Seeds of Deception* is one I recommend that exposes industry and government lies and informs us about the safety of the genetically engineered food we're eating. We have to seek information about the food we give our children in order to make wise purchases. We need to find out how we can protect ourselves and our family. Be sure to *read all labels.* Some infant formula contains GMO ingredients.

Sugar is being put in everything. Beware, some salt has sugar. According to the US Department of Human Services, added sugars show up on food and drink labels under the following names: anhydrous dextrose, brown sugar, cane crystals, cane sugar, corn syrup, corn syrup solids, crystal dextrose, evaporated cane juice, fructose sweetener, and fruit juice. A name that can be seen on so many items is high-fructose corn syrup (HFCS). Why should we be concerned about added sugar and refined sugars? Because we are getting way too much of it, and all those extra, nutritionally empty calories can contribute, in many diets, to problems. Our understanding from research our bodies don't know what to do with HFCS GMO food, so it makes fat. According to the American Heart Association, obesity, type 2 diabetes, and risk factors for heart disease occur. The Center for Science in the Public Interest (CSPI) reports that people who consume diets high in added sugars consume lower levels of fiber, vitamins and minerals, and other nutrients, added sugar may increase the risk of osteoporosis, certain cancers, high blood pressure, and other health problems.

Think about it! We want to be around for a long time in a healthy condition, and we want our children to live healthy lives. We must educate ourselves.

We parents buy the food, and our children need to know we are in control of the food that is purchased. I have had parents tell me their children won't eat anything but pizza and hotdogs. Who buys those items, I wonder? If the child were taught to eat what is cooked for dinner, there is usually no contest. The child knows he or she will be hungry if he or she doesn't eat and won't get another meal until the next day. So the child can make a *choice* to be hungry or eat the good food the parent has provided. Remember, that's called a logical consequence.

Fruit is very sweet. Children can learn to love fruit when things with processed sugar are limited. Because fruit is so sweet, manufacturers have learned to process it and make it concentrated. That's why 100 percent fruit juice is so sweet! It is made from concentrate. The sugar is concentrated. It takes about four medium-size apples to make a cup of juice. Think about the calories. Would you eat four apples at the same time? Probably not.

On the juice jar it might say there are twenty-five grams of sugar in an eight-ounce bottle. This is what blew me away! One gram of sugar equals a quarter teaspoon. So, one teaspoon of granulated sugar equals four grams of sugar. That means that eight-ounce bottle of juice has almost six teaspoons of sugar in it. Can you imagine putting six teaspoons of sugar in an eight-ounce cup of water and having your child drink it? That's when I started saying we will get our juice by eating an orange, apple, berries, etc.

I know this is not a book on nutrition, but that sugar problem is so disturbing to me. If you hadn't heard about the sugar epidemic, I wanted you to be aware.

Just some food for thought!

CHAPTER 15

Joys Outdoors

A parent's awareness of the importance of being outdoors is crucial.

Much of this book has basically been emphasizing what you do with your child at home. However, I hope you will keep the principles in mind and bring them to activities outside. We must especially remember every moment is a teaching moment, and we need to talk to our children *all* the time.

The idea to write this chapter became more urgent when one day my sister in California mentioned hearing a man say, "I'm going to scream if I see another child at Disneyland in a stroller looking at an iPad." You know there is so much to see and experience that the child definitely does not need to be looking at an iPad at Disneyland.

That statement brought to mind the day I was walking in the park and a mother passed by me with a baby in a stroller. The baby had her mom's iPhone looking at it. I wanted to scream and say, "Talk to your baby about what you are seeing, hearing, feeling!" I was motivated to write a chapter teaching ideas for when you go for a walk or to the park, playground, zoo, farm, nature center, and any other outdoor activity.

Erika Christakis, an early childhood educator at the Yale Child Study Center and author of *The Importance of Being Little: What Preschoolers Really Need from Grownups*, cites an alarming trend. A 2011 study published in the *Journal of Pediatrics* revealed that, on weekdays, the average preschooler spends more than four hours in front of a screen.

For older children, the numbers are even worse. According to a 2015 overview of teens, social media, and technology from the Pew Research Center, 92 percent of teens report going online daily—including 24 percent who say they are online "almost constantly."

Christakis said "Active learning (and especially outdoor play in nature) is essential to healthy human development."

As early as 2008 the American Academy of Pediatrics issued a statement saying that *sixty* minutes of daily instructional free play is essential to children's physical and mental health.

I definitely agree with Christakis and the American Academy of Pediatrics that being outdoors is important. That's why I'm writing this chapter. But before we get into ideas for the out of doors, let's look at a few things the American Academy of Pediatrics is saying about screen time. They are realizing that not all screen time is created equal. Computers, tablets, and smartphones are multipurpose devices that can be used for lots of purposes. Designating their use simply as screen time can miss some important variations New guidelines released in October 2016 allow for some screen time for children younger than two and emphasizes parental involvement for all children. These four points summarize their guidelines.

- "Avoid use of screen media other than video-chatting for children younger than 18 months."
- "If you choose to introduce media to children 18-24 months, *find high-quality programming* and co-view and co-play."
- "Limit screen use to 1 hour per day of high-quality programs for children age 2 to 5."
- "Create a family media plan with consistent rules and enforce them for older children."

New research being presented at the 2017 Pediatric Academic Societies Meeting suggests the more time children under two years old spend playing with smartphones, tablets, and *other handheld screens, the more likely they are to begin talking later.*

As the number of smartphones, tablets, electronic games, and other handheld screens in US homes continues to grow, some children begin using these devices before beginning to talk. New research being presented at the 2017 Pediatric Academic Societies Meeting suggests these children may be at higher risk for *speech delays.*

Reports have been made that by their eighteen-month check-ups, 20 percent of the children had daily average handheld device use of twenty-eight minutes, according to their parents. Based on a screening tool for language delay, researchers found that the more handheld screen time a child's parent reported, the more likely the child was to have delays in expressive speech. For each thirty-minute increase in handheld screen time, researchers found a 49 percent increased risk of expressive speech delay."

I suppose these recent findings provide enough information to understand how important it is to monitor screen time for our children.

So any time we cut out something, we need to replace it with something else. This chapter will provide you with some ideas.

Author Richard Louv, author of the book *Last Child in the Woods,* told of a child who said to him, "I like to play indoors better 'cause that's where the electrical outlets are." This might cause us to chuckle, but I want children to love being outside just as much as they love being inside. According to extensive research Louv has conducted, spending time in nature has tremendous benefits, including improved concentration, better motor coordination, improved overall cognitive functioning, and a greater ability to engage in creative play.

Speaking of creative play, it is diminished play in some cases. I have had parents say, "If he doesn't have my iPad or iPhone, he can't think of anything to do." We have to help them think of something. My husband and I never let our children say they were bored. We told them to use their creative ability and think of something to do. Remember when the paint ran out one of my children (the artist now) made her own out of Elmer's glue and food coloring. God has given us awesome brains, and it is amazing what happens when we teach our children to think.

When you go outside, think of the many sights and sounds to bring to your child's awareness. There are many sights, smells, and feelings that can be explored. When I take my children for walks, first, I make them aware of how blessed they are to have legs that can walk, run, skip, and jump. Here are some things to notice as you develop vocabulary in the outdoors.

- Trees: Observe the size of tree (e.g., width and height). Hug a tree. Find the tallest tree. Find the tree that's shaped like the letter Y. Find twin trees. Ask: What is the texture and color of the bark?
- Leaves: Observe the size, color, and shape. Ask, "Is it smooth, rough, or round? How many points does the leaf have?"
- Ground: Observe the soil color. Ask, "Is it wet or dry? Is it rocky, steep, mountainous, or hilly?"
- Grass: Observe the color and blades. Ask, "Are they short, tall, long?" Notice seasonal changes if appropriate in your area. If it is a big, dry field of grass or hay, it's fun to roll in the grass or hay.
- Water: Observe creeks, streams, ponds, rivers, swamps, lakes, and oceans. Ask, "Is it clear? What color is it? Is it small or large? Do you see a waterfall? What do you see?"
- Feel the breeze. Ask, "Is it hot, cool, or cold? Is it blowing the trees? Can you see the wind?"
- Listen to the sounds of nature (e.g., birds, crickets, frogs, wild animals, water in the streams, water rolling over the rocks, etc.).
- Listen to other sounds (e.g., cars, airplanes, someone mowing the lawn, sirens, etc.) Ask, "What do you hear?"
- Sky: Observe the color. Ask, "Is it gray, blue, white, cloudy, or sunny? Can you see any shapes in the clouds?"
- Smells: Notice air smells and leaf smells (e.g., sassafras, skunk cabbage, mint, or whatever leaves that are in your area). Soils have different smells too.

- Flowers: Observe seasonal flowers—colors, shapes, smell, texture, petals, etc. Ask, "How many flowers are there? What kinds of shapes, points, stamen, etc. do you see?"
- Vary what you will talk about on your walks. Make up a song about something you see. The tune "Frere Jacques," "Mary Had a Little Lamb," "The Farmer and the Dell," and "Here We Go Round the Mulberry Bush" are easy tunes that can be used for lots of songs. Remember the songs I made up in the "Joys in the Kitchen" chapter?

Trip to zoo:

- Observe animal habitats.
- Discuss names of animals or learn something new about an animal. Ask, "How many do you see? Are there baby and adults?"
- Categorize the parts of the zoo: mammals, apes, reptiles, birds, etc.
- Observe colors of animals and the scenery around them.
- Ask about what other creatures live in the zoo (birds, reptile, etc.).
- Notice smells.
- Visit botanical gardens or butterfly pavilions.
- Describe the behaviors of creatures.

Beach visit:

- Water: Observe the color and movement. Play in the waves.
- Sand: Observe the color. Make a sand castle.
- Sky: Observe the color. Ask, "Does it look far or close?"
- Wind: Observe the temperature and wind speed. Ask, "Is the wind blowing a lot or a little?"
- Smell: Ask, "Is there a smell? What does it smell like?"

Farm:

- Animals: Discuss names, colors, shapes, sizes, various diets, etc.
- Farm workers: Observe farmers, helpers, etc.
- Farm equipment: Observe tractors, mowers, and plows.

- Farm Buildings: Look at the barn (Ask, "Who lives in the barn?"), silo (Ask, "What goes in the silo?"), chicken coop, pens, stables, etc.
- Animal helpers: Look for horses, dogs, etc.
- Animals that provide food: Observe chickens, cows, pigs, goat, lamb, etc.
- Animals that provide things to help: Talk about lambs (wool), chickens (eggs), cows (milk and cheese), etc.

It doesn't matter where you are. Many of the same concepts can be taught.

Children benefit from the sensory experience of time in nature, including all of the sights, scents, sounds, and textures they can experience when they are outside.

The feeling of the wind on your face can initiate teaching about science and movement of the air. Making children aware of the sounds of various songbirds or any other sounds develop their auditory abilities, which prepares younger children for phonics in school. I listed some sounds above that we sometimes take for granted and can bring to awareness when outdoors.

During your outdoor experience, include gratitude breaks, remembering to thank God for our eyes to see, noses to smell, ears to hear, and ability to feel things, including the wind. We want to draw our children's minds to God, the Creator of our entire beautiful world. Periodically ask, "Who made the trees, the birds, the grass, and so on?" You get the idea—acknowledging God in all things! Be sure to bring out the beauty you see. Enjoy yourself! When you delight in learning, your child will too.

Trying to remember all the things to do may seem laborious at first, but just take one day at a time. Let yourself be free to explore and become more aware of your surroundings. Think about the benefits you also gain by moving.

Hippocrates said, "Walking is a man's best friend."

When you take your child outdoors, you not only show you are a good parent, but you are also benefiting: getting exercise and fresh air and improving your relationship with your child.

Creation Healthy Life Guide—You Were Made for a Garden says, "Experiencing nature is an important pathway to human health and well being ... The more technology we embrace, the more nature we need."

Parenting is a journey, and it takes work. Enjoy your journey.

Epilogue

It has been quite a few years since I started this book. It seems that it was not until now that I could really write about how it is when all of your children fly out of the nest. I can't use the term *empty nest* because my husband always says, "It's not empty. I'm still here." That is true, so I decided to call it, "Flying out of the nest." When my last child was getting ready to leave, I can't even describe the feeling. I remember when she was born. My last child was ten, and my husband and I had decided to have one more even though I was forty-two years old. Priska decided to come a few days early, but the labor was a breeze and my bouncing baby came quickly. All of my three other children were in the labor room. We were amazed when the doctor was cleaning the baby and she was crying naturally. When her dad said, "It is all right Priska. They are just cleaning you off," she stopped crying. Cold silence hit the room. The doctor looked at my husband and said, "Keep talking!" Priska did not make another sound while her dad talked. We had learned that a baby can hear in the womb very early in the pregnancy, so every night Bill would read to the baby from the Bible.

I stayed at home with this baby and taught her kindergarten at home. Priska seemed to grow up fast. In elementary, middle school, and high school, she went to magnet schools for the gifted and talented. She got a scholarship to NYU and graduated from NYU cum laude in broadcast journalism and linguistic anthropology. Priska is an exceptional young lady now living in California working for National Public Radio (NPR). She is still doing what she loved as a child.

I miss her, but I know the things I have shared with you in this book I did with her. I trust that she will find much success and happiness.

Parenting is a journey, and it takes work! Now I am enjoying my two grandsons and am looking forward to new experiences as I continue this journey as a grandmother.

Enjoy your journey. Time goes by so fast. They will be grown before you know it.

Parenting is the most important job you will ever have!

Visions

This book has presented lessons, insights, information, concepts, guides, tools, and examples on how to raise our gifts—children.

I conclude this book with a vision of what the world can become when these lessons are applied and lived on a daily basis.

Consider the things you have experienced as part of the laboratory to experiment on the various ways we can interact to live and be the best parents we can be.

Go forth and apply the teachings, and bring about the vision of a world where parents, teachers, and grandparents work collaboratively to raise gifted, confident, happy children.

I imagine a future of twenty-first-century parents whose focus and emphasis are on their awesome roles and responsibilities. I see parents with communication tools that express unconditional love to their child and develop dynamic relationships in their families.

I see parents managing technology to ensure that relationships are the priority over technology and make a conscious effort to determine what influence technology will have on their family's lives. Technology will be used to enhance lives rather than dictate lives; used to improve learning to obtain new information, not just waste time; and used to make children's lives richer, not dependent on technology to find happiness. These parents realize the detrimental effects technology has on our children, including vocabulary (profanity) that is learned, gun violence, lack of respect, inappropriate behavior, decreasing their attention span, and overstimulation.

Words like, "Leave me alone. Get out of my way. Go watch the TV or go play with your video games, iPads, smartphone, computer, Wii, or Xbox," will cease, and quality time activities will occur, incorporating children into whatever needs to be done.

I see a mother getting ready to do the laundry, and her little five-year-old comes to her and says, "Mommy, will you play Spiderman with me?" She responds by saying, "Sure, come on. You and Spiderman can help with the laundry. Will you and Spiderman make sure the white clothes are all together? I'm so glad you're here. I really needed your help."

We will no longer hear any news of children hurting their pets, siblings, or parents. These gifted children relish in knowing they are loved and have a greater purpose in life.

There will be parents who are careful to never compare their children with others. They know and understand their children's personalities, spiritual gifts, and modes of learning and talents and strive to guide their children in the way of their giftedness.

I see parents that are aware of the power of words and realize they can determine the destiny of their children.

I visualize parents developing lasting relationships and teaching life skills to raise children who become gifted and responsible adults. The life skills include teaching words like *thank you*, *please*, and *may I* to their children. Then these children will carry this information with them all through their lives into the next generation.

Because of what has been learned, these parents know they are their child's first teacher and won't depend on Nana or the daycare provider or teacher to teach their child. They are equipped with skills to teach and prepare the children for further education.

I see homes and marriages that are loving and kind, and parents and children live together in harmony. I see husbands and wives getting along and working together to discipline their children with love.

There are no more cases where our children's hearts have hardened because they have been hurt so much that they refuse to love and feel. But children will know what it means to be loved unconditionally.

This book is the answer to many problems that come our way as parents. My vision and imaginings are real. The application of these principles enhances the joys of parenting. Generation after generation will make the world a better place because this generation remembered children are gifts from God and will choose to train them up to be what God made them to be.

I come to this picture and vision based on my years as a teacher of small children, being a parent and one who teaches parents. It is my joy to see parents smile and say, "There is joy in parenting, and I thank God for my gift."

References

American Academy of Pediatrics. *Handheld Screen Time Linked with Speech Delays in Young Children*. Research presented at Pediatric Academy Society Meeting, 2017.

'Amoreaux, Ray L. *Four Parenting Styles*. Goodyear, AZ: Victorious Christian Living International, Inc., 2006.

Appelbaum, Maryln. *How To Listen So Kids Will Talk*. Sugarland, TX : Appelbaum Training Institute, 1995.

Blitchington, Pete, PH.D, and Cruise, Robert, PH.D. *Understanding Your Temperament: A self-analysis with a Christian viewpoint*. Berrien Springs, Michigan: Andrews University Press, 1979.

Christakis, Erika. *The Importance of Being Little: What Young Children Really Need From Growups*. New York, NY: Penguin Random House, 2017.

Cline, Foster and Fay, Jim. *Parenting With Love and Logic*. NAVPress. com, 1990

Creation Health Life Guide. *You Were Made for a Garden: Experiencing nature is an important pathway to human health and well being*. Maine: Early Childhood Development Team, 2014.

Dyer, Wayne: "When you change the way you look at things, the things you look at change."

Gothard, Bill. *Model on Spiritual Gifts*. Illinois: Institute in Basic Youth Conflicts Inc, 1979.

Holy Bible, King James Version. Nashville: Thomas Nelson Publishers, 1984.

Holy Bible, New Century Version. Nashville: Thomas Nelson Publishers, 1999

Holy Bible, New International Version. Nashville: Holman Bible Publishers, 1999.

Hippocrates: "Walking is a man's best friend."

Kay Kuzma. *How to Discipline Your Child with Love*. First published as *A Hug, a Kiss, and a Kick in the Pants* Illinois: Life Journey Books, David C. Cook Publishing Co, 1989, 1987.

Littauer, Florence. *Setting the Stage for Your Child's Faith*. First published as *Raising Christians—Not Just Children*. Dallas, TX: Baker Publishing Group,1988.

Littauer, Marita. *Wired That Way*. Grand Rapids, MI: Revell, 2006.

Littauer, Marita. *Your Spiritual Personality*. CA: Jossey-Bass A Wiley Imprint, 2005.

Louv, Richard. *Last Child in the Woods: Saving Our Children from Nature-deficit Disorder*. New York, NY: Algonquin Books, 2015.

Max Lacado: "You were made on purpose for a purpose."

McNelis, Deborah. www.braininsightsonline.com

Miranda Rule: "Once a word is spoken, it cannot be retrieved."

Neely, Bill. *The Gift of Criticism*. IN: WESTBOW Press, 2017

Oscar Wilde: "Be yourself, everyone else is taken."

Pew Research Center, "92 percent of teens report going online."

Plato: "Music gives a soul to the universe, wings to the mind, flight to the imagination and life to everything."

Savage, John D. Min.. L.E.A.D.Consultants, Inc.. OH: 1988

Songbook. *Little Voices Praise Him*. Hagerstown, MD: The Review and Herald Publishing Co.

Smith, Jeffrey. *Seeds of Deception*. VT: Chelsea Green Publishing, 2003.

Appendix

Creative Ideas for Prayer Time

- Prayer partners: Pray by twos.
- Hand squeeze: Hold hands in circle. Each person prays silently, and when finished you squeeze the hand you are holding.
- ACTS Prayer: Pray one-sentence prayers following this formula: A=adoration to God, C=confession of guilt, T=thanksgiving, S=supplication (asking God for something).
- Scripture prayer: Read a scripture that is a prayer, or read a scripture and have your prayer centered on that theme.
- Popcorn prayer: This does not involve eating. The words popping out of your mouth remind one of corn popping. Families can decide to see how many things they can think of to thank God for and say it quickly. It doesn't matter what the prayer is. It's just saying it quickly like corn popping.
- Prayer collage: Cut out pictures of things you are thankful for and glue them to a large sheet of paper, making a collage.
- Prayer walks: Decide to walk around the neighborhood and pray for each house.
- Alphabet prayer: When the children are old enough to know the alphabet, start with A and see if they can think of a word that describes God or something that God made that starts with that letter. For example A—apple God made, or A—almighty, amazing, awesome God.
- M&M prayers: Dump a handful M&Ms on a plate. Let each child choose one color—yellow, brown, green, or red. The colors determine what is prayed about.

- Yellow: adoring God (pray about what you like about God)
- Brown: confession, telling God sorry
- Green: thanking God
- Red: making special requests of God (praying for something you want God to do or give you)

- Lord's Prayer chain: Get in a circle and say the prayer a phrase at a time. Or for older children, cut out strips of paper and have them write phrases of the Lord's Prayer on them and put them in the correct order, making a chain. Tape the strips together.
- Sensory prayers: This prayer helps to reinforce something you're talking about in a Bible lesson or scripture. Chew a piece of fruit, feel a feather, rub a furry real or stuffed animal, be creative, and enjoy praying to God.

We teach our children about God in everything we do. Remember, wherever we are, it's worship.

Additional Activities to Reinforce and Remember the Spiritual Gifts

Matching game

- Draw a line to match the characteristic to the gift (see insert).
- Put the characteristics under the name of each gift (list provided).
- Put names and characteristics on separate sheets of construction paper. Pass out paper. Each person finds his or her match. Song/Game to reinforce the gifts of essence.

The Gift of Prophecy	The Gift of Service	The Gift of Teaching	The Gift of Exhortation	The Gift of Giving	The Gift of Leadership	The Gift of Mercy

List of Spiritual Gifts

Proclaim truth and expose sin	Meets needs of other	Clarify the truth	Promote spiritual maturity	Entrust assets and maximize results	Plan ahead and complete tasks	To be with those who suffer
Must express themselves	Difficulty saying no	Likes lots of data, detail	Sees the root of the problem	Gives to answer prayers	Visualize final results	Deeply loyal to friends
Loyal to the truth	Short range projects	Uneasy with subjective truth	Turns problems into benefits	Prone to give secretly	Alert to details	Empathy for those in pain
Deep desire for justice	Needs approval and appreciation	Very thorough	Prefers face-to-face sharing	Encourages others to give	Completes tasks quickly	Attracted to people in distress

List of characteristics for Spiritual Gifts

Spiritual Gift Matching Game

The Gifts of Essence

(Draw a line to match the characteristics of the gifts)

The Gift of Exhortation	Proclaim truth and expose sin
The Gift of Giving	Meets needs and free others
The Gift of Service	Clarify truth and validate information
The Gift of Teaching	Stimulate faith and promote maturity
The Gift of Prophecy	Entrust assets and maximize results
The Gift of Mercy	Plan ahead and complete tasks
The Gift of Leadership	Remove distress and share burdens

Instructions: This game will improve memorization of the main characteristics of each gift. Draw a line from gift to characteristic.

We All Fit Together Like A Puzzle
We All Need Each Other

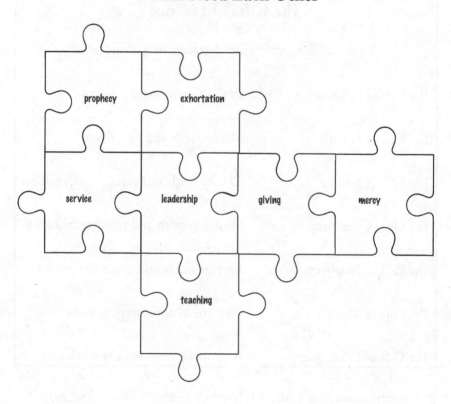

Puzzle

- For younger group: Color, then cut the puzzle and instruct the children to put the puzzle back together. They learn to sight-read the words.

- For older group: Have a puzzle for two groups of children. Each group begins putting the puzzle together at the same time. The group that finishes first wins. Repeat. The way each child responds to the competition will give you clues as to what his or her gift might be.

- Sing the song below: Using a group of seven children, six form a circle around one child. The child in the center turns around with eyes closed and finger pointing as the other children sing the song. After the question, the child being pointed to answers. The child should be given a name of a gift if help is needed. Then that person gets in the middle. This continues until all have a turn.

  - Song: Sing to the tune of "Have You Ever Seen a Lassie?" If you don't know it, Google it.

- Words: There are seven gifts of essence, of essence, of essence. There are seven gifts of essence, who will name one?

Teaching the Memory Verse Using a Multisensory Approach

This is a review of the concepts learned in the chapter on the five senses. Maximum learning takes place when we incorporate all sensory avenues. When auditory, visual, tactile-kinesthetic, and experiential (including olfactory and gustatory) learning styles are included in teaching, students are engaged, have fun, and are able to apply concepts to their lives. Therefore, in this seminar we provide instruction on teaching the memory verse using the multisensory approach. We want our children to be able to see, hear, feel, and apply God's Word to their lives.

When teaching memory verses, here are a few ideas using a multisensory approach.

Objectives

- To have children who love God's Word and hide it in their hearts!
- To provide opportunities for children to learn scripture using all of the five senses God gave them to learn.

Supplies Needed

- color markers
- construction paper
- index cards (4x6 or 5x7 for younger children)
- CD player (Steve Green's scripture CDs)
- illustrated song banners
- sign language illustrations
- bouncing ball

The following ways are suggestions for using a multisensory approach to teaching the Bible verse. All ages can benefit from these activities.

- Introduce the Bible verse by clapping each word (every syllable), including the Bible text.
- Clap hands first and then say, "Let's pat our knees and say the memory verse. Now let's tell our shoulders, elbows, legs, etc." For

younger children, show them how to cross the midline to pat the shoulders

- Write the memory verse out on index cards (4x6 for older children and 5x8 for younger children). Lay the cards out on the floor as you say each word. Have the children repeat after you. The young children learn to sight-read the words quickly. For older children, mix up the words and have the class put the memory verse in the right order.

- While the words are on the floor, sing the scripture song and point to each word as you sing.

- Have each child take turns bouncing a ball to the words in the memory verse. Younger children may need you to put your hand on the ball to help bounce. If the class is too young, make a circle on the floor and roll the ball to each other as one of the words in the memory verse is being said. Help them to remember.

- Get in a circle in chairs or on the floor. (This is great for families that are blessed with lots of gifts—children.)
  - This is played like "Duck, Duck, Goose," but as the children touch each head, they are saying the memory verse. Begin with a child tapping on the head and saying the memory verse. (All of them are saying the memory verse together.)
  - The child whose head is tapped on the last word in the Bible text gets up and chases the tapper. If the chaser tags the tapper before he or she reaches the open seat, the tagger has another turn. If not, the chaser now becomes the tapper. By the time the game is finished, the whole class knows the memory verse.

- Perform scripture song using sign language (online videos).
- Put memory verse on banners.
- Pass out strips of paper with each word of the memory verse. Have the children stand in the correct order, and then have each child say his or her word (for older children).
- Give out a sheet of white eight-by-ten paper and have the children or the child illustrate the memory verse (for older group). There is no right or wrong answer. The pictures they draw are what the memory verse means to each individual.

- Food to taste or fragrances that would enhance the meaning and memory of the memory verse are encouraged. For example, if the memory verse is, "He (God) gives food to every living creature," have a plate of different fruit to taste. In my book, *Thank You God for My Food*, you will find a scripture for every food learned. In the back of the book find "Activity Go Alongs" with recipes and activities to enhance learning.

Other Books by Edwina Neely

Thank You God for My Body

www.createspace.com/900002058

Thank You God for My Food

www.createspace.com/1000251964

Contact Edwina at
edwinaneely@gmail.com

About the Author

Edwina Ruth Grice Neely is a wife and mother of four children. She is a parent, educator, seminar presenter, author, and entrepreneur. She feels she has been put on earth to nurture the souls of God's gift—children. She is a magnet for children. She can take a crying baby from a mother and calm him or her down. When she goes on walks, children come up to her and smile or talk to her. There is a special connection she has with children.

She has a MA in speech pathology and audiology and post-graduate credentials in early childhood education. As a speech pathologist, Edwina's work with children made her consciously aware of the impact a parent has on a child's development. This led her to stay at home with her children, and for fourteen years she directed a home-based daycare and preschool.

Her love for children and passion to help parents in their parenting journeys led her to develop a parent-teacher partnership program providing seminars to parents of her students. She has now founded Parent Assistant Resource (PAR) for Success. This is a support system for families, schools, and churches—the answer to a parent's cry for help!

She is author of two children's books, *Thank You God for My Body* and *Thank You God for My Food*. She has coauthored a parents' devotional, *Help! I'm a Parent: Christian Parenting in the Real World*.

Just for fun, Edwina has a baking business. She enjoys making wholesome breads, cakes, and pies. This includes gluten-free and sugarless items. It gives her utmost joy to bake for parents, friends, and family for holidays, birthdays, and other special occasions.

Edwina is also a vocalist and plays clarinet in her husband's band. They take their music to nursing homes, church fairs, and school festivals to bring joy to many lives.

During Edwina's forty-plus years of teaching, she has had the opportunity to experience the lives of many children. She has seen parents struggling with their relationships, parents who wanted help in discipline, and parents who wanted help in just understanding what makes their children behave the way they do. Some were frustrated, helpless, and embarrassed, and some wanted insights, tools, and encouragement to be better parents. So she reached out and started a parent-teacher partnership program with monthly meetings.

Even though Edwina is no longer in the classroom, she still has the passion to help parents. This book is an extension of her, providing a guide, insights, practical ideas, joys to experience, and lessons to warm the heart, encourage, and perhaps challenge all who are involved in the parenting journey. She wants parents to know that they have received a gift from God. This gift comes prepackaged and unique, with gifts, talents, abilities, personalities, and modes of learning to be discovered as the child reveals who he or she is. When children know what their gifts are, they are confident and happy to discover the many opportunities their abilities offer. This is a guide to aid parents in raising gifted, confident, and happy children.

Edwina believes parenting is the most important job in the world. Even though parenting can be challenging, it can be a happy journey. Yes, you have received a gift! Embrace the thought and enjoy the journey!

Song: "I'm Special"

I'm Special

Edwina Grice Neely / Arr. by Kenneth D. Logan